SELF-REFLECTION IN THE ARTS AND SCIENCES

SELF-REFLECTION IN THE ARTS AND SCIENCES

by
Alan Blum and Peter McHugh

HUMANITIES PRESS
ATLANTIC HIGHLANDS, N.J.

First published in 1984 in the United States of America by
Humanities Press Inc., Atlantic Highlands, NJ 07716

©Copyright 1984 by Humanities Press Inc.

LIBRARY OF CONGRESS CATALOGING IN PUBLICATION DATA

Blum, Alan.
  Self-reflection in the arts and sciences.

  Includes bibliographical references and index.
  1. Self-knowledge, Theory of. 2. Hermeneutics.
3. Languages—Philosophy. I. McHugh, Peter, 1929—
II. Title.
BD450.B53   1983   126   83–7062
ISBN 0–391–02877–4

MANUFACTURED IN THE UNITED STATES OF AMERICA

Acknowledgements

This little book seeks to construct for the reader a conversation which raises the question of how to conceive of the theorist as a social actor in the strongest possible (principled) way. As such it builds on our previous work and attempts to develop it in certain directions.

Today, the argument for a strong version of theorizing has to live with the opinion that all claims to theorize have equal validity as an irrevocable condition of its environment; it must accept the moods of constructionism, "unlimited semiosis", misology, et al as the mood(s) of the day. Yet mechanical and dogmatic responses are less compelling than an analysis which discloses the argumentative structure of all pictures of theorizing as the beginning of a narrative oriented to its own principled character.

We would like to thank our students, friends and supportive colleagues over the last few years. Special thanks are due to Stephen Karatheodoris who allowed us to freely use part of his dissertation (as we acknowledged) at certain points in this work.

Contents

Introduction

Our problem is self-reflection. We will seek here to develop a statement of our work—its scope, objectives, and limits—by addressing at the same time certain parts of the past and present literature in the field.[1]

That our formulation of the problem is inseparable from other relevant writing is hardly a novel intellectual plan. Nevertheless, because the literature is often complex and occasionally esoteric in its significance for self-reflection, an ordinary inventory of sources and issues would not suit our purpose. One reason for this is that the literature we discuss raises questions concerning the very problem of what it is to discuss a literature— that is, it raises the question of the nature of interpreting, translating, and reflecting upon texts. To inventory would be to already have accepted that an inventory is an adequate version of what the problem of discussion is. Of course it is unavoidable that we all do speak from some position, but the descriptive and generalizing format required by the exegetical survey of issues and texts accepts in advance some version of the possibility of neutral discourse, a possibility whose terms we would like to revive for discussion.[2]

Consequently, we shall discuss our sources with the intention of isolating central issues as we conceive of these issues to emerge from a consideration of the sources. Other interests could produce other issues. We can only accomplish our task by reconstructing these sources *as if* they constitute a conversation about the problems of interest to us. Because a certain violence of interpretation is unavoidable—indeed desirable—we do not promise a disinterested review of opinions on the subject of self-reflection, but rather attempt to provide the grounds or foundations of our intellectual problem *through* a discussion of sources. In this way, we seek to reconceptualize the literature in order to develop the significance of our particular problem as an interest that is valuable.

We contend that it is the character of language that provides for the differences among intellectual positions as expressed in "the plurality of principles and methods which make . . . refutation . . . a simple exercise of exposing absurd meanings which statements have when interpreted from other points of view than they were intended to express."[3] An inventory masks the interested character of its formulation of other positions behind a descriptive facade, as if the defects of other positions are found in the inadequacies of their basic principles and methods or in the misuses to which these principles and methods are put. But the relationship between positions is itself a problem of method and principle in that every position exemplifies its own method and principle in its very judgment of others.[4] Yet, if an adequate review is not to succumb to relativism—to the opinion that a source can only report upon itself and that judgment inevitably assimilates to itself and hence destroys the integrity of what is being judged—it must recollect the sources and positions it reviews as a way of making available its own methods and principles as an interested application and exemplification of its own value and aim. This problem will constitute a central focus for our project.

Organization of the Discussion

After a preliminary statement of the problem, we will seek to situate our project by providing for its antecedents in (1) the critique of the positive sciences inspired by many thinkers, of whom we select Marx and Husserl as examples, (2) the reformulation of this critique as a conception of the limits of language in the works of Wittgenstein, deSaussure, and Heidegger, (3) the consequences of this conception of language for the problem of self-reflection as it evolved in the sociological tradition (of, for example, Weber and Simmel) as a concern with the social character of knowledge, and (4) as it developed and was reshaped in contemporary writings such as ethnomethodology, critical theory, and semiotics.

Issues in the problem of self-reflection will be collected progressively as a feature of the action of the narrative. While these issues have been understood historically in terms of the distinction between theory and practice, as symptoms of the "linguistic turn " they will be restated as posing the question of adequate discourse, i.e., the question as to the possibility of speaking well and not arbitrarily about conventions even and inasmuch as such speech depends upon these selfsame conventions.

Exposition and Self-Reflection

> The forms assumed in the exposition of philosophies make use of the
> values and means of communication of existing communities . . . [and]
> . . . seek to create new communities based on fundamental . . values . . .
> and philosophy even in its most sober and scientific form is a kind of
> conversation which turns attention . . . to principles recommended for
> acceptance.[5]

Any exposition—including the present one—originates on the ground of
principles and methods—that is, it is oriented. This in itself is vacuous until
we recognize that *what* any exposition is oriented to, "even in its most sober
form," is recommending and proposing its *own principles and methods*.
Any exposition is necessarily self-centered; it "turns attention" to itself by
recommending itself.

Furthermore, we must assume of any such exposition that its centering
upon itself (no matter what it speaks about) is oriented, that it is not
compelled but done for reasons, and that the principal reason for so
centering is that the exposition understands its expository practice as desirable,
valuable, and good. Thus, any exposition says of itself through its very
occurrence that its expository methods and principles are good.[6]

We note here an opportunity to begin to grasp the nature of self-
reflection. It is not distinguished by its self-centeredness, since all speech
can be seen as a response to, and as a way of affirming, principles and
methods of adequate speaking, whether or not the speaker is so aware. Self-
reflection can be tentatively distinguished as speech that orients to its center
(to its origin or principle), as speech that orients to the way it centers itself.

We can even go further and say that what an inquiry inquires about (its
concrete topic) is not its analytic end, because we locate that end in its aim
to create acceptance for its principles. These principles constitute principled
ways of formulating and conceptualizing a topic and can be seen as an
authoritative way of discussing or discoursing about a topic. Seen in this
light, the end of inquiry is always an authoritative recommendation for
speaking about a topic, where the topic acquires its relevance as the
medium through which the authority is made transparent. A communicative
end is not merely a "goal" of inquiry, but it also impregnates the very
constitution of inquiry as its foundation.

This is not to say that inquiry needs to speak about its authoritative
method of speaking by enumerating its procedures and assumptions, but
rather that its routine accomplishment as a speech shows what it is speaking

for (its conception of ideal discourse, of an ideal speaker) as an integral part of what it says. So we can begin to think of self-reflection as speech that understands itself (which understands what it *shows*) in this way.

In one sense, the antagonist of self-reflection is speech that loses sight of this fact, the fact that it shows an authoritative and hence particular way of speaking as its idealization. For example, such speech might universalize itself by treating its particular recommendation—its prescription—as if it were natural or self-evident. Such speech *acts as if* the sense and value of its discourse are settled by consulting its referents or by recapitulating its behavioral accomplishment. Criticism in this mode then takes the form of responding to technical problems, problems that could be solved by developing new means of approaching referents or new means of recapitulating behavioral accomplishments.

In this way, the foundation of the inquiry in its discursive value—in the tacit and idealized end of authoritative speaking that it recommends—is concealed because the speech is treated as if it were oriented technically (to solve the problems of its correspondence with objects or its coherence with history) rather than discursively. In contrast, our formulation of self-reflection must provide for an actor whose theorizing is rooted in a particular and decisive discursive aim. In this sense, the actor will be an ideal speaker who is oriented toward making the grounds of his speech in principle available and intelligible. Although the substantial expression of such a speaker could vary greatly, his formal interest in making such substantial ends contestable need reveal a common aim regardless of particular differences.

The Self-Reflective Actor as an Ideal

We require a strong version of social action from which we can develop a conception of self-reflection and of the self-reflective actor as an ideal orientation to the world. By "ideal" we do not mean goals-to-be-reached, but a standard to which the actor orients as necessary and decisive. The "problem" of self-reflection will then emerge in the form of the necessary decisions such an actor has to meet, decisions of sense, passion, rationality, and the like. Such an actor has to be constructed to exhibit not only the competencies but also the founding commitment required in any solution to those decisions or problems that we ascribe to self-reflection as an intelligible course of action.

The idealization of self-reflection most familiar in the positive sciences, and the authoritative standard for all the modern arts and sciences, is the image of self-reflection as technology and of the self-reflective speaker as a technologist.

The technologist personifies a particular form of rationality: He is constructed to follow rules and to connect rules to acts by organizing his behavior in accord with rules. The technologist tends to disregard the way in which the rules that he follows are rooted in the deep need to ground the validity of these rules in a principled conception of good discourse. He tends to act as if (to speak as if) his rules (which reflect particular circumstances and needs) are universal. In this sense, he is abstract about his principles, because he treats his rules as if they originated necessarily or inevitably and not through the oriented and motivated work that draws upon a sense of the competition between principled ways of discoursing.

We shall develop the argument that the technological version of self-reflection rests upon a very particular conception of language and of the relationship between language and the world, a conception that leads the technologist to identify adequate discourse as speech that takes for granted the very question of adequate discourse, even as it speaks about adequacy and validity. That is, the technologist treats the question of adequate discourse as if it were a technical problem, because he conceives of language either as a means for connecting private thoughts to public things, or as a multiplicity of public usages, each of which is interchangeable in terms of value.

Preliminary Statement

One characteristic of the evolution of the human sciences[7]—a characteristic that is integral rather than incidental—is its inevitable self-reflection upon its theories and interpretive procedures. This self-reflection is not an accessory feature of the growth of the arts and sciences but a ground and presupposition of their development and a continuous topic of their organized concern. As ground, the problem of self-reflection functions as a sometimes tacit but always decisive limit upon the intelligibility of much of the work that is done. As a topic, the problem is addressed in each and all of the disciplines through various and specialized interests in theory, method, and procedure.[8]

We understand the various arts and sciences as social enterprises that operate under the auspices of socially defined limits, rules, and objectives.[9] Regardless of the particular form that concerted self-reflection assumes between and within disciplines, and regardless of the disputes that regularly occur among practitioners and divide them, this range of practices shows a unitary need to adjust to such limits (whether as topic, resource, or constraint) as a necessary problem to which each and all must orient regardless of their differences. This is to say that all the arts and sciences are concerned to establish self-reflection upon their theories and procedures *in some form* as a continuous and legitimate enterprise.

In every discipline, self-reflection is addressed as a topic in works on method and philosophies of correct procedure; it is used as a resource when practitioners follow rules to carry out their work; it functions as a constraint or limit in providing often tacit terms and conditions of the very thought and speech of the discipline and, thus, is a foundation for thinking about procedures canons, and rules.

Let it be noted that the self-reflection that occurs variously in the different arts and sciences is not engaged only and exclusively by the theorists, philosophers, or mandarins of the disciplines, but is necessarily displayed in the varieties of mundane and standard studies and researches developed as a feature of the ordinary work and life of these sciences. To paraphrase Kuhn, commitment to self-reflection is not esoteric because subscription to limits, rules, and objectives is displayed in the whole range of ordinary projects and procedures that constitute the discipline.[10]

We know that the various arts and sciences identify themselves on the basis of the subjects they appropriate;[11] but the point is that in each and every appropriation is some omnirelevant and omnipresent conception of limit and possibility that is respected as a constraint and with which these practitioners seek to comply. Following Max Weber, sociologists have spoken about the "normative order" of a discipline as itself a social fact to which action orients and by which it is governed in its course.[12] For the practitioner-as-actor the "problem" of self-reflection is transparent even in its tacit compulsion upon him as the normative order that sanctions and provides for the enforcement of canons of intelligibility and correctness as socially organized conventions. This order is also available in the oriented self-corrective work of these disciplines and in the employment of standards of criticalness, relevance, and adequate discourse. Sometimes practitioners seek to describe such an order explicitly, but more often it pervades the work in the form of unacknowledged limitations to which they necessarily subscribe. Despite practitioners' senses of priorities in substantive problems within any discipline, it is safe to say (and we shall assume such) that the problem of the normative order of adequate procedures stands to these various substantive problems as a limit relates to a topic or as a foundation stands to a superstructure.[13]

In a sense, the problem of self-reflection—now tentatively understood as our way of making reference to the relationship between the practitioner and the normative order of adequate procedure—has been a primary topic of concern for those practitioners engaged in self-reflection upon the work of their disciplines. This concern has issued in countless inventories of principles, technical recipes, and canons of procedure in each of the human sciences.[14] However, it is also true that in their mundane actions—in identifying problems, in making routine decisions, in deciding what can and cannot be done or what is worth doing, in criticizing, evaluating, and forming their very work—practitioners show in socially organized ways their subscription to binding and "valid" senses of principle, technique, and procedure.

Because the problem of self-reflection is not a substantive problem at all, but rather a condition for the very existence and practice of each of the human sciences; its emergence is a necessary feature of the evolution of these sciences.[15] We symbolize this "problem" through the figure of the normative order of adequate procedures presupposed as an environment of knowledge to which practitioners must orient. One important consequence of these moves (of our moves here) is our formulation of self-reflection in accord with Weber's conception of social action as "action oriented to an order and governed thereby in its course."[16]

The fact that self-reflection can be conceived as an instance of social action points to what it shares with all human practices; indeed, it points to its roots in ordinary language or in the "life-world." Nevertheless, that self-reflection is not extraordinary in this sense should not obscure the recognition that, like any social action, it has its own distinctive aim, excellence, and value. In part, our task will be to formulate self-reflection as a course of social action while taking into account both its similarity to, and its difference from, other practices.

This is to say that while our acknowledgement of self-reflection as a course of social action gives us the opportunity to study self-reflection sociologically—that is, through the procedures of empirical social science—those very procedures are topics and problems of our narrative on self-reflection. Consequently, our interest will not be in *describing* the behavior of self-reflection (even while we acknowledge its possibility as such a describable topic); our concern is to invent (construct) an idealized version (an order) of self-reflection as a rational action to which the inquiry can orient.[17]

Some Implications

The focus of our project upon the "problem" of self-reflection implicates us in this very problem.[18] This is to say that the work of this monograph must stand as a feature of the self-reflection that accompanies the growth of the human sciences that we seek to reformulate in the monograph, and that we use as a resource for the formulation.

Because we ourselves are a product of the debate upon self-reflection and of its influences, we do not promise a neutral review of issues or a survey of positions. Our concern is to isolate in an intelligible way certain distinctive threads that promise to suggest opportunities for our own development and specification of a very particular program with its own specific limits, objectives, and directions of interest.

Our discussion can in no way be disinterested, because it is a feature of the very problem that it intends to formulate. This is only to say that we must already have in mind some intended solution (or an image of possible solutions) to the problem of self-reflection as anticipated in our conception of self-reflective action as rational. A version of such a rational course of action grounds our discussion; it guides our collection of issues by ruling our selective and often eccentric readings of the materials and our organization of the conversation, i.e., of the narrative itself. This is to say that the way in which we converse about the problem of self-reflection is in some sense decided by our conception of adequate discourse (of adequate self-reflection). Though we cannot endlessly recapitulate arguments for our decisions, this does not mean that we cannot speak strongly enough to invite argument or to make argument possible. To say that our discussion cannot be disinterested is not to say that it cannot be rational; but here, too, we require the reader's support to suspend his notions of adequate discourse as "disinterested" in order to let our narrative develop.

Consequently, our discussion must operate at several levels simultaneously. To open up our formulation of the problem of the self-reflective actor requires continuous acceptance of certain unexplicated and unanalyzed assumptions that we must use as resources in the course of the narrative. Moreover, an adequate "reading" of the narrative at any one point often requires hard work on the part of the reader in consulting the text, both retrospectively and prospectively, in order to establish the relevance and sense of the narrative. Finally, the uses that the reader has in mind and that he brings to the text must be continuously adjusted, translated, and reformulated as he encounters the narrative in order for him to allow the narrative to grow on its own terms.

All this is to say that if this formulation of self-reflection is itself an instance of the action of self-reflection, the text—the narrative—must be encountered as a course of social action guided by its own aim and relevances and oriented in a motivated way to some version of the normative order of self-reflective action as a standard of adequate discourse.[19] If our narrative *is* such an action, the fact that its referents, decisions, allusions, and assignments of sense are arguable is not an essential problem, because any social action is defeasible, i.e., can be otherwise. What *is* essential is that the ground (the foundation) of the narrative be available as a discussable topic for a rational conversation and that the "point" of the narrative—the "deep need" it expresses—be made available as a value that is intelligible.

This is why we are not in a position to inventory the issues reflected by the problem of self-reflection and why we have no interest in establishing general conclusions about the problem. We are not doing an exegetical survey upon all opinions that have been expressed on the topic, nor are we doing a summary or synthesis of the historic discussion. Such a task would be to write the history of philosophy, but this is not our interest.

For example, the reader should in no sense accept as authoritative the discussion of self-reflection sustained by philosophy in its epistemological or metaphysical forms, or by the sciences in the form of "philosophy of science." While we draw upon contributors to that discussion in crucial ways, we do not accept as our limits its categories, relevances, and rules, because they often presuppose problematic conceptions—particularly of the relationship between language and the world—that we need to address.

Similarly, the self-reports of particular arts and sciences upon their theories and procedures become useful at various points in the narrative, but only through their status as the formulative work of practitioners. This is to say that we do not see these results as *necessarily* binding and valid. Paraphrasing Marx, we might say that if practitioners' formulative work in the arts and sciences tends to be limited by technical interests in their objects, then philosophy tends toward an abstract conception of adequate discourse, which has grown on the soil of its indifference to the particular roots of self-reflection in social action. Of course, there are exceptions to *this* generalization, and we draw upon the work of distinguished philosophers and social scientists at crucial points.

What we are saying is that our formulation of self-reflection as the problematic relationship between an actor and his social environment must not be seen exclusively in terms of the canons of either adequate sociological description or adequate philosophical argument. This is not to protest evaluation. It is only to recommend that our interest in developing a conception of self-reflection as social action is necessarily directed toward inventing ways and means of appraising work that are not necessarily adumbrated by those traditions. In part, our project is animated by a desire to recollect work that was done within those traditions as a responsible resistance to their conceptions of limit, objectives, and end. So, if we intend to develop and cultivate a framework for adequate discourse that does not presuppose many of the received conventions of these historic disciplines, we can still be responsive to their interests as loci or contexts in which they developed. Our project might then be read as a narrative that seeks to make available the intelligibility and rationality of *different presuppositions,* while yet conceding that our enterprise is itself nourished in essential ways by the projects from which it seeks to depart.

NOTES

1. Strictly speaking, we are not dealing with a "field," since the issues and sources we discuss transcend such designations. We are actually engaged in constructing a "field."

2. Cf. T. Kuhn's remarks in I. Lakatos and A. Musgrave, eds., *Criticism and the Growth of Knowledge* (Cambridge: Cambridge University Press, 1970), p. 268. "Languages cut up the world in different ways and we have no access to a neutral sub-linguistic means of reporting."

3. R. McKeon, "Philosophy and Method," *The Journal of Philosophy,* XLVIII, no. 27, p. 659.

4. Ibid., p. 660.

5. Ibid., p. 657.

6. When the exposition recapitulates itself as rules, it says that these rules are normative for doing the exposition as it is done. The principle is always tacitly assumed as the reason for wanting to do it in that way when it can be done otherwise.

7. We use the terms "human sciences" and the "arts and sciences" interchangeably, in accord with the original Greek notion of a science and an art.

8. In part, the work of unraveling the meaning of "self-reflection" is the topic of this monograph. Suffice it to say for now that it has—in our use—nothing to do with idealist or introspective usages, but refers to the analysis of language.

9. This is to say that an art or a science is essentially a social organization, a typical and regular action governed in its course by a perceivedly valid and binding normative order. F. Kaufmann, *Methodology of the Social Sciences* (New York: Humanities Press, 1944), p. 67.

"A norm is a maxim that governs the behaviour of the person who seeks to comply with it. However for the person who appraises human behaviour in terms of the norm, it is a criterion for the correctness of this behaviour. In other words, it is for him a definition, or part of definition, of "correct behaviour for particular types." Correct thinking is defined in terms of agreement with the rules of logic just as correct speech is defined in terms of agreement with the rules of grammar or legal behaviour in terms of agreement with given norms of positive law.

The scientist must not make a decision arbitrarily . . . he must have grounds for each decision, i.e., must show that it is permissible [correct] in terms of the presupposed rules of scientific procedure. In other words, the rules of scientific procedure state the conditions for exemptions from the general prohibition against changing the corpus of sciences.

As soon as it is undertood that concepts such as "correct," "grounded," "control," "confirmation," are relational concepts presupposing the system of procedural rules, these conclusions become a matter of course. But this point is seldom clearly understood because truth and falsity are regarded as immanent properties of propositions. Consequently the controls are interpreted as means of discovering which of the two truth values is possessed by the proposition." Although Kaufmann is speaking about the social organization of the empirical sciences, what he says here holds true to some degree for each of the arts and sciences.

10. The dispute between Kuhn and Popper on "normal science" (Cf. I. Lakatos and A. Musgrave, eds., *Criticism and the Growth of Knowledge* (Cambridge: Cambridge University Press, 1970), addresses this issue. Essentially, Popper claims that an analytic version of science requires a formulation of the rationality of the inquirer—the scientist—as stronger than Kuhn is willing to allow, as if Kuhn takes his bearings from a typification of scientific practice that does not sufficiently idealize it in terms of its highest possibility. In contrast, Kuhn argues that he uses "normal science" as a way of referring to the normative order of science; insofar as that order is understood as the normatively ordered requirements of typical scientific work, it can collect both extraordinary and normal scientists. In sociological jargon, Popper thinks that Kuhn's formulation cannot provide for deviance, whereas Kuhn correctly points out that even deviance presupposes a commitment to the intelligibility of the limits being transgressed. Yet, Popper senses the way in which Kuhn's depiction of the normative order of science, in terms of various notions like "paradigms" and "frameworks," tends to sociologize the perceivedly valid and binding character of this order out of existence by equating rationality with intelligibility and "consensually shared frameworks."

11. In part, the history of disciplines is an epic tale of the conquest and appropriation of "objects." Durkheim, *Rules of Sociological Method* (Glencoe: Free Press, 1964), does this for sociology. A more recent effort can be found in L. Althusser, *For Marx* (London: Allan Lane, 1969).

12. M. Weber, *The Theory of Social and Economic Organization* (Glencoe: Free Press, 1947), pp. 87-125.

13. Perhaps this relationship is clarified by Kaufmann's distinction between preferential rules and basic rules, where basic rules provide grounds for scientific decisions in particular cases, and preferential rules refer to "proximate goals of every scientist *qua* scientist." F. Kaufmann, op. cit., p. 67.

14. Most of the works on theory and method in the various disciplines are of this nature; they formulate rules to follow deemed authoritative and desirable, or they restate the procedures of esteemed researches as maxims of conduct.

15. This is to say that the problem of self-reflection makes reference in the first instance to the tacitly organized grasp of the discipline as *what* it is, as an enterprise that is intelligible and identifiable. For example, the various works in literature, in physics, and in anthropology all presuppose among practitioners the possibility of a rational enagement with the "objects" of literary, physical, and anthropological inquiry, and so they presuppose that what is quested after is already in hand as a determination and limitation upon what is to be done—that is, as a feature of the self-reflection upon the action of doing it.

16. That inquiry is action testifies to the fact that it necessarily originates on the ground of an oriented and acquired grasp of what inquiry is as an identification of how to proceed in order to perform the action of inquiry.

17. This is to say, first, that we treat self-reflection as action rather than behavior (in Weber's terms), conceding that our oriented distinction here is itself an instance of the action

rather than the behavior of self-reflection; second, in a sense to be developed, we require of any conception of action that it acknowledge its constructive character by representing what it studies as a rational idealization instead of seeking to establish general statements describing its empirical occurrence. Winch describes this difference.

> The difference is . . . analogous to that between being able to formulate statistical laws about the likely occurrence of words in a language and being able to understand what was being said by someone who spoke the language. The latter can never be reduced to the former; the man who understands Chinese is not a man who has a firm grasp of the statistical probabilities for the occurrences of the various words in the Chinese language. Indeed he could have that without knowing that he was dealing with a language at all; and, anyway, the knowledge that he was dealing with language is not itself something that could be formulated statistically. "Understanding," in situations like this, is grasping the point or meaning of what is being done or said. This is a notion far removed from the world of statistics and causal laws; it is closer to the realm of discourse and to the internal relations that link the parts of a realm of discourse. P. Winch, *The Idea of a Social Science and its Relation to Philosophy* (London: Routledge & Kegan Paul, 1958), p. 150.

18. Cf. M. Heidegger, *Being and Time,* trans. J. Macquarrie and E. Robinson (New York: Harper & Row, 1962), pp. 24-25.

> Every inquiry is a seeking. Every seeking gets guided before-hand by what is sought . . . any inquiry, as an inquiry about something, *has that which is asked about* . . . In investigating questions—that is, in questions which are specifically theoretical—what is asked about is determined and conceptualized . . . in what is asked about there lies also that which is to be found out by the asking: this is what is neatly intended: with this the inquiry reaches its goal . . . inquiry as a kind of seeking, must be guided beforehand by what is sought.

19. It should be clear that our work here—the writing—is an instance of social action. What we say is not self-evident; we have purposes, make decisions, invoke rules, and gloss other options in ways that are oriented and decisive. The self-reflective character of writing remains to be demonstrated in the writing itself, since it is dependent upon how we display in our narrative an oriented grasp of the possibilities we exclude.

Critique of the Positive Sciences

Husserl's Critique: Consciousness as an Accomplishment

In his critique of the positive sciences, Husserl did not seek to deny their achievements or successes. He granted the productivity of the positive sciences. His critique was directed to the mode of self-reflection of these sciences.

> Thus all the occasional ("even philosophical") reflections which go from technical (scientific) work back to its true meaning always stop at idealized nature; they do not carry out the reflection radically, going back to the ultimate purpose which the new science, together with the geometry which is inseparable from it, growing out of prescientific life and its surrounding world, was from the beginning supposed to serve: a purpose which necessarily lay in this prescientific life and was related to its life-world. Man (including the natural scientist), living in this world, could put all his practical and theoretical questions only to *it*—could refer in his theories only to it, in its open, endless horizon of things unknown.[1]

What self-reflection was limited by was its indifference to the actual and concrete life-world in which its own world takes shape.

> This actually intuited, actually experienced and experienceable world, in which pratically our whole life takes place, remains unchanged as what it is, in its own essential structure and its own concrete causal style, whatever we may do with or without techniques. Thus it is often not changed by the fact that we invent a particular technique . . . what do we actually accomplish through this technique? Nothing but prediction extended to infinity.[2]

13

The self-reflection of the sciences is abstract, i.e., artificial, because the discourse in terms of which it formulates itself as a practice in the world—as a living practice—actually simplifies that development by "dressing it up" or clothing it in a "garb of ideas." These ideas are not adequate for depicting the development that they intend to represent in any but an elliptical way.

> In . . . natural-scientific mathematization, in the open infinity of possible experiences, we measure the life-world—the world constantly given to us as actual in our concrete world-life—for a well-fitting *garb of ideas,* that of the so-called objectively scientific truths. That is, through a method which . . . can be really carried out in every particular and constantly verified, we first construct numerical indices for the actual and possible sensible plena of the concretely intuited shapes of the life-world, and in this way we obtain possibilities of predicting concrete occurrences in the intuitively given life-world, occurrences which are not yet or no longer actually given . . . mathematics and mathematical science, as a garb of ideas, or the garb of symbols of the symbolic mathematical theories, encompasses everything which, for scientists and the educated generally, represents the life-world, dresses it up as "objectively actual and true" nature. It is through the garb of ideas that we take for true being what is actually a method—a method which is designed for the purpose of progressively improving, *in infinitum,* through "scientific" predictions, those rash predictions which are the only ones originally possible within the sphere of what is actually experienced and experienceable in the life-world.[3]

What the self-reflection of the sciences reveals is an image of its practice as naive, as alienated from its essential mode of being in the world, and thus it reveals an image of the scientist as one who has no commitment to the life-world; he is seen as unoriented and so as originally innocent of any connection to life itself.

> Thus, no one was ever made conscious of the radical problem of *how* this sort of naiveté actually became possible and is still possible as a living historical fact; how a method which is actually directed toward a goal, the systematic solution of an endless scientific task, and which continually achieves undoubted results, could ever grow up and be able to function usefully through the centuries when no one possessed a real understanding of the actual meaning and internal necessity of such accomplishments. What was lacking and what is still lacking, is the actual self-evidence through which he who knows and accomplishes can give himself an account, not only of what he does that is new and what he works with, but also of the implications of meaning which are closed off . . . i.e., of the constant presuppositions of his (own) constructions, concepts, propositions, theories. Are science and its

method not like a machine, reliable in accomplishing obviously very useful things, a machine everyone can learn to operate correctly without in the least understanding the inner possibility and necessity of this sort of accomplishment? But . . . was science, capable of being designed in advance, like a machine, without an understanding which was, in a similar sense, complete—scientific? Does this not lead to a *regressus in infinitum*?[4]

But why is it necessary to refer our concepts back to the life-world? Because the life-world is not something we have left, it is not "behind" us, as something to which we can return. It is omnipresent and omnirelevant. We are not dealing with a dualism here, as if there is consciousness *and* the life-world. The life-world is the language in which we live. It is not that our consciousness refers to this world as if it exists apart from consciousness itself: rather, consciousness is consciousness *of* and *in* the life-world.

Yet Husserl's critique evolves as a feature of those very possibilities that science's reflection upon itself had opened up, for now it was possible to make transparent the connection of the sciences (and their mode of self-reflection) to the life-world.

Now at last it was possible and necessary to become aware of the fact—which had remained completely unconsidered in these sciences—that the life of consciousness is a life of *accomplishment*: the accomplishment, right or wrong, of . . . meaning, even sensibly intuited meaning, and all the more of scientific meaning.[5]

Marx's Critique: The Social Production of Consciousness

Marx had already distinguished two types of philosophers, empiricists and idealists, as perfect examples of those who sunder the relationship of consciousness to life.[6] If idealism develops the "active side" (the idea of an actor), which materialism suppresses, it still treats this actor "abstractly," as if his relationship to the world is formal and asocial. Neither empiricism nor idealism understand action as "real sensuous activity," i.e., "subjectively."[7] In Marx's terminology, empiricism and idealism each in their way are said to reify one part of this relationship—the relationship of consciousness to life—at the expense of the whole. The "whole" stands for the relationship *as* a relationship.

Consciousness is therefore from the very beginning a social product and remains so as long as men exist at all.[8]

Apparently, the relationship between consciousness and life is explicated through the conception of consciousness as "a social product." To say that consciousness is a "social product" is, in Husserl's idiom, to say that it is an "accomplishment." Furthermore, to say that consciousness shows its roots in "life" is to say that it can only be understood as an accomplishment, as a social product.

To what does "life" make reference? Marx speaks of "reality," "real actors," "real forces," "material conditions," and the like. Yet "life"— human life—occurs when men produce their difference from what is nonhuman.[9] If "life" then appears to be identical with the production of consciousness (including the consciousness of the difference between man and nature), it had best be understood as identical not to consciousness but to *production*. To relate consciousness to life is to understand life as a production, as an "accomplishment." To see the life in any event—to see the interpenetration of action and life—we need to envisage the constitution of things; we need to envisage a thing as a course of action that is assembled.

Consciousness originates in "real individuals, their activities and the material conditions under which they live, both those they find already existing and those produced by their activity."[10] We are accustomed to hear this as a reference to "economy," but why not understand it as depicting what Husserl called the "life-world"? Marx criticizes the philosophers because they segregate consciousness from life—that is, they treat consciousness rather than life as the limit(s) of what is real. In the same way, Husserl criticizes scientists for their forgetfulness of science's roots in the life-world.It is this motive that produces the dualistic conception of life and consciousness as an obstacle to adequate self-reflection upon their interpenetration.

> Galileo abstracts from the subjects as persons leading a personal life: he abstracts from all that is in any way spiritual, from all cultural properties that are attached to things in human *praxis*. The result of this abstraction is the things purely as bodies; but these are taken as concrete real objects, the totality of which makes up a world which becomes the subject matter of research. One can truly say that the idea of nature as a really self-enclosed world of bodies first emerges with Galileo. A consequence of this, along with mathematization, which is too quickly taken for granted, is (the idea of) a self-enclosed natural causality in which every occurrence is determined unequivocally and in advance. Clearly the way is thus prepared for dualism . . . the conception of the new idea of 'nature' as an encapsuled, really and theoretically self-enclosed world of bodies soon brings about a

complete transformation of the idea of the world in general. The world splits, so to speak, into two worlds: nature and the psychic world . . .[11]

In the first thesis on Feuerbach, Marx refers to the "chief defect(s)" of materialism and idealism. He was not objecting to the sort of error we customarily associate with the word "defect." He was repudiating a form of life that spawns an insurmountable cleavage between theory and practice.[12] The critique of idealism and materialism contained in the *Theses* neither casts doubt on unsure premises nor exposes false conclusions; it reviews the very criteria of truth and falsity upon which these traditions rest. Marx accomplishes this review through a radical rethinking of the role that social life plays in the formation of consciousness. For Marx, both idealism and materialism (rationalism and empiricism) pass over the social grounds of consciousness in silence, but they are not, on that account, *merely* defective misrepresentations; for both theoretically display the type of sociation to which they conform. In other words, Marx detected a sense in which the illusory cleavage between thinking and acting presupposed by idealism and materialism accurately depicts the alienated and defective form of life that he took to be supporting and infusing them. Therefore, Marx's demand that we abandon this illusory cleavage is irrevocably coupled to his repudiation of the form of life that *requires* such an illusion.

The *Theses on Feuerbach* is neither a rational nor an empirical critique, but a dialectical explication of the practices upon which rationalism and empiricism rely. Marx's analysis goes beyond what either of these epistemologies says to the grounds that both leave unsaid. He formulates these grounds as *praxis,* conceiving of *praxis* as the ensemble of social interactions that underlies the various authoritative forms of self-reflection that consciousness affirms as its "theoretical" limits.

At bottom, thought Marx, what warrants our certainty is neither the self-evident proposition sought by Descartes nor the incorrigibility that Bacon and Locke tried to impute to consciousness. Giving grounds and marshaling evidence come to an end, but the end is neither an apodictic assertion nor an incontestable sense impression; it is our social life—activity that lends credence and cogency to our thinking.

Marx felt that we arrive at the truth of a matter when our thinking penetrates and illuminates the character of our conduct. Since our conduct is essentially social, its illumination requires an understanding of how it is rooted in value—in conceptions of ends, or limits, in methods and decisions that draw upon interested and oriented conceptions of excellence. However, consciousness conceals its social character by evoking auspices such as "nature" or the "essence of man." Consciousness then offers resistance to itself, to its own (internal) possibilities for understanding itself as social.

Thus the ultimate value relevance of life (of consciousness) is concealed by notions such as "nature" and the "essence of man." For example, when we say that it is *natural* to act in a certain way, the word "natural" serves to conceal the *optional* and *ethical* dimension of our conduct. We are prone to use it in lieu of addressing the *agathon* (the good) for the sake of which we act. Marx's rejection of the classical British economists is, in part, based upon the fact that they *begin* with a version of "natural economic man" that remains an unexamined resource of their analysis. "Nature" and "essence of man" palliate our sense of responsibility by preventing us from subjecting our conduct to scrutiny. To understand consciousness as social is to appreciate the essential conventionality of our consciousness. Because "it could be otherwise," that it must be accomplished in the way it is can be adequate only *given* the (social) decision to reject other ways in which it could be done. This rejection (not necessarily explicit) is part of the sense of its being done in the way it is.[13]

In response to empiricism, Marx says that consciousness relinquishes responsibility for the decisive and judgmental constitution of the datum. In contrast, idealism "develops this active side abstractly." This is to say that Marx rejects the idea of an "innate" consciousness because it presupposes an image of the life-world as "the inner, dumb generality which unites the many individuals naturally."[14] Such a formulation is "abstract" because it conceals the way(s) in which consciousness as a social product is accomplished as a result of the particular circumstantiality that is the life-world.

Think of "life" or "life-world" as a metaphor for the idea of the necessary origin of action in the material particularity of social existence.[15] Consciousness—if by that we mean thinking and speaking—is always an accomplishment or product. How then is this product "social"? To this we could imagine an answer: What is social is constituted; it is organized and accomplished under the auspices of ends, of a sense of value.

> The . . . meaning of the pregiven life-world is a subjective structure, it is the achievement of experiencing, pre-scientific life. In this life the meaning and the . . . validity of the world are built up—of that particular world, that is, which is actually valid for the individual experiencer. As for the "objectively true" world, the world of science, it is a structure at a higher level, built on pre-scientific experiencing and thinking, or rather on its accomplishments of validity. Only a radical

inquiry back into subjectivity—and specifically the subjectivity which ultimately brings about all world-validities, with its content and in all its pre-scientific and scientific modes, and into the "what" and the "how" of the rational accomplishments—can make objective truth comprehensible and arrive at the ultimate . . . meaning of the world. Thus, it is not the being of the world as unquestioned, taken for granted, which is primary in itself; and one is not made to ask what belongs to it objectively; rather, what is primary in itself is subjectivity, understood as that which naively pre-gives the being of the world and then rationalizes or . . . objectifies it.[16]

What is accomplished results from work; through the exertion of labor, an action is constituted or put together. What is accomplished is achieved as a doing that completes or terminates. The successful performance of the action depends upon what is normative for the action—that is, upon adopting and following the ways in which the action is done.[17] An accomplishment presupposes the existence of such a norm, presupposes that there is something to do that would be correct to do here. To say action is an accomplishment is to say that its occurrence is ruled by a sense of what it is to do the action at all ("it is a subjective structure, it is the achievement of experiencing"). That which it is to do the action at all we could speak of as its *telos,* its end or value; it is the necessary condition of failure for the act[18] in the sense that without it the act would not *be.*

When Husserl talks of consciousness as an accomplishment, or when Marx speaks of it as a result of production, each depicts it as a social product in that it is seen to be oriented, to be ruled by some conception of what it is to do the action. We speak of that which rules this accomplishment as an end or aim. The end is not segregated from the action as some "goal" it seeks to accomplish; indeed, the end is essential and internal to the doing of the action as the action that it is. Aristotle says:

Every art and every inquiry, and similarly every action and pursuit, is thought to aim at some good.[19]

Yet the action is not guided and directed by itself. The conception of the end that orients the action is rooted in "life," in the "life-world." Philosophers have often tended to speak as if consciousness directs itself, but Marx and Husserl say that this is to forget its origin in life. "Life" now becomes transparent as the actual and sensual relationship of man to his world. It is in this relationship that the idea of how to do what is done arises as a practical and concrete feature of the relationship itself. In fact, what the relationship is (what it means) in the first instance is the particularity of sensuous and concrete valuing. To say that consciousnes originates in life is not to suggest anything "new"; it is to say that consciousness will formulate itself reflectively only when it grasps its essential interpenetration with practice. This means that consciousness must grasp how its deciding and valuing is essential to it.

> Modern confusion about the relative status of facts and values results from a misunderstanding or exaggeration of the classical distinction between theory and practice. One finds very clearly in Aristotle, and more ambiguously in Plato, recognition of the difference between an attempt to see mentally 'how things are' (theory) and an attempt to ascertain the relative degrees of excellence of the various modes of human conduct (practice). For both thinkers, however, these two kinds of mental activity are related precisely by what one could call 'the logical structure of the world'. Of course, 'logical' here means something quite different from the meaning attached to the term by its contemporary admirers. The Greek word *logos* means both speech and reason. To the Socratic philosophers, the world is 'logical' and 'reasonable' because it provides us with a basis for speaking meaningfully about the relative merits of the various human activities. The leap between theory and practice, then, is not an abstract argument in epistemology . . . but the nature of man as the animal who both speaks and acts. There is then a reasonable basis in nature for distinguishing and responding to the *unreasonable*.[20]

Marx says of Feuerbach that he wants to establish "consciousness . . . of this fact," of the particular fact or condition, whereas more truly "it is a question of overthrowing the existing state of things."[21] In the "existing state of things," the roots of consciousness in practice are forgotten, and *that* is what must be overthrown. When consciousness forgets its origin in practice, it acts as if it governs itself, as if it were independent and autonomous. Consciousness tends not to see its ends as residing in its lively and interested beginnings.

The attempt of consciousness to treat itself as evident and self-governing is shown in its effort to account for itself—to provide a logos—that would make no reference to its lively (practical) origin. Consciousness would then be consciousness "of this fact"; that is, it would describe itself as an achievement that is asocial. Such a logos would describe how consciousnes works without reference to its end, aim, or point.

> Contemporary man desperately needs a rational interpretation of reason. We are unable to explain to ourselves in a rational way the point to our success, and consequently the difference between success

and failure. . . . Instead (we have) been furnished epistemologies, or technical discussions of how reason works. Even these technical discussions, for all their genius, have been theoretically compromised by the inability to ask why reason is working.[22]

This self-report of consciousness upon itself will only be a "technology" because it treats its origins as self-evident.

The new conception of the world of bodies, self-enclosed as nature, and the natural sciences related to them, the correlative conception of the self-enclosed souls and the task, related to them, of a new psychology with a rational method according to the mathematical model—all this had established itself. In every direction rational philosophy was under construction; of primary interest were discoveries, theories, the rigor of their influences, and correspondingly the general problem of method and its perfection. Thus knowledge was very much discussed, and from a scientifically general point of view. This reflection on knowledge, however, was not transcendental reflection but rather a reflection on the *praxis* of knowledge and was thus similar to the reflection carried out by one who works in any other practical sphere of interest, the kind which is expressed in the general propositions of a technology.[23]

To say that consciousness treats its ends technologically is to say that it treats its objectives as if the only question of interest pertains to their actualization or realization, and as if the only solution to that question requires a plan or program that specifies conditions in the realization of ends without respect to their nature. Consciousness tends to assimilate its concern for its relationship to life to the question of method.[24]

When left to its own resources, consciousness can only envisage as its ideal a standard of discourse the achievement of which is governed exclusively by general conditions. Here the logos that consciousness provides for its own accomplishment is representated as a self-report upon the conditions under which it occurs as what it is, as consciousness. Such a discourse ultimately represents the accomplishment of consciousness as a result of rules and methods.

Insofar as a course of action—the accomplishment of consciousness—is described through its methods of coming to be as it is, the description formulates conditions that are general and not particular to its occurrence. What is particular to the occurrence of consciousness is that it grows on the soil of a particular and "subjective" (though not ephemeral) relation to the world. This is to say that it need assume an interest in its own formation, in its own appearing to be as it is. The end of consciousness—its self-image as an intended accomplishment—governs its coming to be both as a standard and a source.

> When we say how an action is done (how to act) what we say may report or describe the way we *in fact* do it . . . but it may also lay out a way of doing or saying something which is to be followed.[25]

The general methods proposed in the description of how a self-governing consciousness is accomplished—of its method—can be taken as binding rules if we want to accomplish the action (if we want to accomplish consciousness). In treating action as intelligible, we have to assume a rule follower, because from the point of view of the life-world—of the subjectivity and value of the actor's involvement—general conditions must be seen as rules to follow in accomplishing the action. This is to say that the life-world is introduced into the formulation of consciousnes only insofar as its accomplishment can be translated from a description of general methods into a formulation of rules. Yet even the idea of rules glosses the dependence of consciousness on the notion of the life-world. The idea of life-world says that we need to envisage any occurrence as a self-assertive orientation to occurring itself.

Theoreticity

The conception of consciousness as a social product then necessarily requires that it be treated as that action an actor wants to do. That this actor is oriented means only that he is situated in the life-world, that his wanting to do as he does is subjective, is impregnated with value.[26]

Yet, how could an inventory of rules reproduce his doing what he wants to do? If the rules governing the accomplishment of consciousness had the status of causal laws that hold for every man, it would be causally impossible for any man to break one of the rules, and rules that no normal man can break are not rules that can guide the behavior of any normal man.[27] This is to say that to have a rule it is necessary that a man should be able to break the rule, and to formulate an actor as a rule follower is to include as an essential feature some conception of his awareness of the rule as a rule, some conception of his sense of the rule as a choice rather than as a necessary constraint.[28] A formulation of rules must be more than a generalization that *is* a rule, because it needs to refer in its description to the actor's orientation to rule.

The dog who balances sugar on its nose in response to its master's command has no conception of what it would be to respond differently (because it has no *conception* of what it is doing at all). Hence, it has no alternative to what it does; it just responds to the appropriate stimulus.[29]

The critiques by Marx and Husserl recommend that any self-reflective comprehension of the relationship of consciousness to life requires a formulation of consciousness as a social product or accomplishment as its way of preserving the "subjective interest," or oriented character, of consciousness as a social action in the life-world. We have gone further by formulating this recommendation as an injunction to represent the event(s) of consciousness as the action of following rules. While it can be argued that our "reading" was not adumbrated by Husserl or Marx and is not to be retrieved from their texts, we, in contrast, would stipulate this reading as an intelligible conceptualization of the ideas of "subjective interest" and of "life-world."

And yet, we would claim that the depiction of consciousness as rule following, while preserving the necessary notion of "subjective interest," is insufficient for adequate self-reflection upon the relationship of consciousness to life. If the subjective interest of the action—the oriented character of its accomplishment—is conceived as the following of rules, the accomplishment can still be described in ways that affirm science's empirical self-reflective standard as a limit. This is to say that rule following can still be described in ways that suppress the motivated character of social action.[30]

When the self-report of consciousness is represented in the ideal discourse of generalization—whether as statements of method *or* of rules— these generalizations can only formulate an actor who is governed (rather than guided) by causal conditions.[31] This discourse describes regularities as its mode of representing the accomplishment of consciousness *as if* the actor were a dog rather than oriented. The event (the development of consciousness) is brought under general rules without requiring of itself the assumption that these rules *are oriented to* as features of the actor's life-world.[32] Generalization is then achieved by denying the oriented, sensuous, and valued character of the action.[33]

Indeed, the actor's orientation is suppressed whenever an incorrigible foundation for his action is supplied (whether perception, intuition, mind, or concept), because such foundations suggest the necessity of the action as a determinate rather than valued consequence of his following rules. Yet, the fact that rules can be violated—that rules come to an end, that following rules presupposes interpretive work on the part of the actor—shows how the orderliness that general statements ascribe is itself the result of the work of repressing the particularity of the actor's orientation. To avoid seeing the action as technologically necessary (whether as an inevitable outcome of methods or of following rules), we need to imagine the choice that any vision of its necessity still presupposes.[34] The real actor—the motivated actor— does not simply *adapt* to rules, because in his following a rule, he necessarily orients to what it excludes as that which he could do.[35]

Alternative Conceptions of the Life-World

There is a rejoinder to (our formulation of) the critiques by Husserl and Marx. In the *Timaeus,* Plato has Timaeus say:

> An account is of the same order as the things which it sets forth—an account of that which is abiding and stable and discoverable by the aid of reasons will itself be abiding and unchangeable . . .[36]

Some would argue that consciousness (whether philosophy, science or theory) is situated by these thinkers in a 'life-world' that is formulated by them as particular, concrete and sensual. They would say that the life-world so identified is essentially contingent and random and is therefore irrational and dangerous, because any logos, center, or source would have to participate in this irrationality. Here the argument of Marx and Husserl that we have developed as the need of consciousness to recognize the ultimate particularity of the life-world is said to dissolve all speech (including reflection) in the solipsism of isolated life-worlds—in the problem of "subjectivity."

Consequently, it might be said that we have not recognized how our version of the accomplishment of consciousness is incommensurate with certain implications of the critique, implications that suggest different alternatives.

First, perhaps consciousness could be stabilized rather than random if it is seen to be formed by objects that are part of consciousness because they are present to it. Adequate self-reflection in this instance should represent the report of consciousness upon the objects of its own history, formation, and development as a series of (sensory, perceptual, etc.) exchanges. This recommendation produces empiricism, whether as psychology, epistemology, or varieties of descriptive linguistics wherein consciousness is translated as speech.

Alternatively, consciousness could be the particular application of the conceptual possibilities that are intrinsic to it. Adequate self-reflection would here represent the report of consciousness upon its combinatorial or generative possibilities as a series of (cognitive, conceptual, mental, intuitive) transformations. This recommendation produces rationalism and idealism in epistemology and varieties of transformational or "structural" analyses when consciousness is translated into language.[37]

Needless to say, these alternatives are instances of those very forms of self-reflection against which the critique of Marx and Husserl was directed. Those who resist the possibility of self-reflection might suggest that the failure of the 'solutions' to meet the standard set by the critique only affirms the impossibility of the critique. Why set standards than cannot be met, because the irrationality of the life-world (the roots of life in apparently random and particular contingency) appears to make the topic of self-reflection inapproachable and ineffable? However, it still remains for those who do accept some part of the critique to develop an argument that the life-world can be made intelligibile as a topic by reformulating it through such conceptions as speech, ordinary language, "members' methods," the "symbolic or social construction of reality," or the interacting influences of conditions or exigencies upon conduct. That is, they will claim that such a "life-world" is still describable. We will review these attempts further on. Suffice to say for now that they represent various ways of understanding how the (supposedly) irrational life-world can provide all of the resources for a rational (discursive) response ("that there is a reasonable basis in nature for responding to the unreasonable").

Argument

Let us collect our argument to this point by restating the major implications of the critique developed by Marx and Husserl and some possible rejoinders to it.

1. It is said that an adequate comprehension of the relationship of consciousness to life requires a formulation of consciousness as a "social product" or accomplishment. Though this stipulation is arguable, depending upon how action or conduct is conceptualized, we accept it for the purposes of our work.

2. To preserve the character of consciousness as such an achievement, it is necessary to formulate the roots of consciousness in the life-world as an instance of "subjective interest" or "oriented action." This is because of the assumption that any intelligible action might be intelligible to the one who performs it as what he is doing. This assumption is not empirical.[38]

3. Although the "subjective interest" or oriented character of consciousness is a necessary ascription for any conception of consciousness as a course of action, it is not a sufficient condition for adequate formulative work. A variety of "schools of thought" have acknowledged such a parameter while still seeking to describe the action (the accomplishment of consciousness) as a function or result of general conditions external to the action itself. The so-called sociology of knowledge and genetic psychology are two examples that come to mind.[39]

4. It is necessary to depict the oriented action of consciousness as an instance of rule following, with the actor as one who envisages the action's accomplishment as an intelligible and normative construal of how the action is to be done—that is, as an order with which he seeks to comply and which he tends to respect. This conception of the action as rule following is necessary but not sufficient for adequate formulative work, because such action could be described empirically in terms of an association between conventions.[40]

5. Such a formulation cannot depict rule following in terms of general conditions, because that would envisage action as governed by constraints that are compelling rather than inviting, and thus they would violate the previous assumptions.[41]

6. Yet the consistent attempt to follow the previous assumptions as if they were rules for producing adequate self-reflection upon the relationship between life and consiousness appears to lead to an insoluble dilemma. The rules for accomplishing self-reflection seem to formulate self-reflection itself—because of *its* connection to the life-world—as essentially particular and irrational, i.e., as "subjective." Therefore, the project threatens to dissolve in the very subjective interest that it assumes of its subject matter— and so, it is said, in arbitrariness.

NOTES

1. E. Husserl, *The Crisis of European Sciences and Transcendental Phenomenology* (Evanston: Northwestern University Press, 1970), p. 50.

2. Ibid., pp. 50-51.

3. Ibid., p. 51.

4. Ibid., p. 52.

5. Ibid., p. 90.

6. K. Marx and F. Engels, *The German Ideology* (New York: International Publishers, 1947).

7. Ibid., pp. 651–653.

8. Ibid., p. 19.

9. Ibid., p. 7.

10. Ibid., p. 7.

11. Husserl, op. cit., p. 60.

12. These next five paragraphs draw heavily upon S. Karatheodoris' doctoral dissertation, *The Logic and Ethic of Science: A Sociological Exegesis of the Cognitive Grounds of Practice and the Practical Grounds of Cognition* (Department of Sociology, New York University, 1977).

13. S. Cavell, *Must We Mean What We Say* (New York: Scribner's, 1969), p. 22.

The most characteristic fact about actions is that they can . . . go wrong, that they can be performed incorrectly This is not, in any restricted sense, a moral assertion, though it points to the moral of intelligent activity. And it is as true of describing as it is of calculating or promising or plotting or warning or asserting or designing . . . these are actions which we perform, and our successful performance of them depends upon our adopting and following ways in which the action in question is done, upon what is normative for it. Descriptive statements, then, are not opposed to ones which are normative, but in fact presuppose them: we could not do the thing we call describing if language did not provide (we had not been taught) words normative for describing.

14. Marx, op. cit., p. 199.

15. W. Outhwaite, *Understanding Social Life: The Method Called Verstehend* (New York: Allen & Unwin, 1975), p. 111.

Few people would deny, though some would consider it uninteresting, that the starting point of social inquiry is some sort of intersubjective understanding. This is not merely to affirm that ordinary language is the ultimate meta language of any science . . . it is rather that we begin in the . . . talking "every day language" and using "every day accounting procedures."

16. Husserl, op. cit., p. 69.

17. Cavell, op. cit., pp. 22-23.

Descriptive utterances are not examples of normative utterances. Establishing the norm is not telling us how we *ought* to perform an action, but telling us how the action is done or how it is to be done. Contrarywise, telling us what we ought to do is not instituting a norm to cover the case, but rather presupposes the existence of such a norm, i.e., presupposes that there is something to do which it would be correct to do here. Telling us what we ought to do may involve appeal to a pre-existing rule or standard, but it cannot constitute the establishment of that rule or standard.

18. On "necessary condition of failure," see D. Shwayder, *The Stratification of Behavior* (New York: Humanities Press, 1968). Eventually, we shall distinguish this sense of *telos* (as intelligibility) from *arete* (excellence).

19. Aristotle, *Nichomachean Ethics* (New York: Modern Library, 1947), p. 1094a.

20. S. Rosen, *Nihilism* (New Haven, Conn.: Yale University Press, 1969), p. 56.

21. Marx, op. cit., p. 33.

22. Rosen, op. cit., p. 57.

23. Husserl, op. cit., p. 92.

24. As we shall develop the argument in subsequent sections, this means that the limits of the inquirer's interest—of the interest of self-reflection—is in the intelligibility of speech (its rules) rather than in its principled character. In his distinctive idiom, Parsons recognized this as the crucial "instability" of utilitarian conceptions of action; that is, by treating ends as unanalyzed (as random), they assimiliated the question of value to "conditions" of action. See T. Parsons, *The Structure of Social Action* (New York: McGraw-Hill, 1937).

25. Cavell, op. cit., p. 15.

26. P. Winch, *The Idea of a Social Science and Its Relation to Philosophy* (London: Routledge & Kegan Paul, 1958), p. 58.

I want to say that the test of whether a man's actions are the application of a rule is not whether he can *formulate* it but whether it makes sense to distinguish between a right and a wrong way of doing things in connection with what he does. Where that makes sense, then it must also make sense to say that he is applying a criterion in what he does even though he does not and perhaps cannot, formulate that criterion.

27. Cf. J. Bennett, *Rationality* (London: Routledge & Kegan Paul, 1969), p. 17.
28. Winch, op. cit., p. 32.

... The notion of following a rule is logically inseparable from the notion of making a mistake. If it is possible to say of someone that he is following a rule that means that one can ask whether he is doing what he does correctly or not. Otherwise there is no foothold to his behaviour in which the notion of a rule can take a grip; there has been no *sense* in describing his behaviour in that way, since everything he does is as good as anything else he might do, whereas the concept of a rule is that it should enable us to evaluate what is being done.

29. Winch, op. cit., p. 65.
30. For example, by conceiving of the action empirically, one can hypothesize or predict certain probable consequencs, and in this way, one could count the success of the forecast as evidence of the adequacy of the conception.
31. See Bennett, op. cit., on the distinction between rule governed and rule guided.
32. Note that this assumption is an analytic stipulation rather than an empirical designation.
33. Generalization is achieved only by divesting the (idea of) action of its oriented character, which is (in our terms) an *analytic* requirement of its intelligibility.
34. This choice is *analytic*. See Winch, op. cit., p. 65.

The moral life is 'conduct' to which there is an alternative ... this 'alternative' need not be consciously before the agent's mind ... it must be something which *could* be brought before his mind. This condition is fulfilled only if the agent could defend what he has done against the allegation that he ought to have done something different.
Or at least he must be able to understand what it would have been like to act differently ... Understanding something involves understanding the contradictory too: I understand what it is to act honestly just so far and not farther than I understand what it is to not act honestly. That is why conduct which is the product of understanding, and only that, is conduct to which there is an alternative.

35. We must reiterate that this necessity is analytic, that it is ascribed by the inquirer as an essential condition of social action.
36. Plato, *Timaeus*, 28b.
37. Cf. F. Kaufmann, *Methodology of The Social Sciences* (New York: Humanities Press, 1944), pp. 18-19.

Here ... we find ourselves confronted with the question: How are the elementary meanings given? Two answers have been offered in the history of philosophy that appear to be exclusive of each other. One is that they are given by 'experience,' ultimately reducible to some state; the other, that they are given by 'reason' ... prior to all experience. According to the latter view, the faculty of reason or intuition is innate, an essential character of the soul. The simile corresponding to the first view is that of the soul as a blank sheet of paper on which experience writes ... according to the second doctrine it may be compared to a marble block disclosing certain veins that cannot be neglected by the artist ... Unforunately the issue has almost always been obscured by the failure to distinguish between logical and genetic priorities. The philosophical problem is not to give a causal explanation of the appearance of ideas in the soul (mind), but to clarify the presuppositions implicit in thought and to arrange them in their proper logical order. In describing a sense experience, we have to characterize it in general terms and thereby to presuppose meanings . . . Any attempt therefore to determine the meaning of . . . a particular sense experience is futile. An "ostensive definition" is not a definition. Nor do we fare better if we refer to 'reason' or 'intuition' as the source of universals. No such faculty can be characterized without presupposing the meaning of its performance.

38. The action has (analytically) to be conceived as intelligible to the one who does it—he is required to act under the auspices of the formulation of the action.

39. They then confuse analytic requirements of the (conception of the) action with its empirical designation.

40. This is to say that if conventions are agreements, they can be described and traced to chance, and their interrelationships can be treated as an empirical topic for social analysis, which is exactly what sociology does. See Leo Strauss, *Natural Right and History* (Chicago: University of Chicago Press, 1953).

41. The requirement of rule-guided (rather than rule-governed) action is that the actor orients to the rule *as rule* and, hence, to knowing that its being done entails constructive and oriented work (interpretation).

The Social Order Problem:
The Possibility of Language

If it is claimed that the intent to preserve respect for the subjective interest of the actor necessarily leads to the dissolution of inquiry into subjectivity, we suspect that this charge is intelligible only when reflection is conceived as a particular type of social relationship between a self and another, and thus in terms of one limited image of the connection between language and the world.[1] In order to develop our argument properly, we need to examine various conceptions and images of the relation of language to life.

The Life-World as Language

The concept of life or the life-world that we identified in the critique developed by Marx and Husserl made reference to the ground and source of consciousness; we understand that grounding as a way of referring to the pervasiveness of language, to the limits of language as the limits of life. It is not that consciousness *depends* upon the life-world as if that world could be an "antecedent variable"; rather, consciousness is inexplicable except as a demonstration of the pervasiveness of the life-world as an affirmation of the limits of language. That everything is settled within language—including the relationship between consciousness and the life-world, and including the problem of language itself—means that language is engaged in recollecting itself, that this is its reflection upon itself.[2]

While we can speak endlessly about the relationship between language and the world in the sense that our sentences can make endless representations of that world, what connects our sentences to the world is settled within language—within the world. That which connects our language to the world is not discovered by our language 'in' the world as if the world lay outside of our language; it is within language itself that such matters get decided.[3] Cavell puts the point clearly:

> We forget that we learn language and learn the world together, that they become elaborated and distorted together, and in the same places. We may also be forgetting how elaborate a process the learning is. We tend to take what a native speaker does when he looks up a noun in a dictionary as the characteristic process of learning language. (As, in what has become a less forgivable tendency, we treat naming as the fundamental source of meaning.) But this is merely the end point in the process of learning the word.
>
> When we turn to the dictionary . . . we already know everything about the word, as it were, but its combination: we know what a noun is and how to name an object and how to look up a word . . . we are all prepared . . . what seemed like finding the world in a dictionary was really a case of bringing the world to the dictionary. We had the world with us all the time, in that armchair; but we felt the weight of it only when we felt the lack of it in it.[4]

Therefore, in terms of the interests of our project, we see that what we know about the world is possible only because we can think and speak meaningfully about the world.[5]

Yet, for our purposes, thinking and speaking ought not to be segregated. One of our principal assumptions stipulates that our thinking about the world (our consciousness) always occurs as an instance of a discursive relationship, that the apparent externality of the various referents for our words is only grasped as such through an organized and socially standard way of ascribing intelligibility, i.e., through language itself.[6]

Our program for self-reflection then necessarily has its roots in a conception of language and of the self-reflective actor/speaker as a language user. Our first assumption should be amended as follows: What we know of the world is possible only because we can meaningfully speak about the world. Thus, in the first instance, consciousness occurs as an exemplification of speech and programs for self-reflection (upon the relation of consciousness to the world) are—from our perspective—always part of a discussion on how we speak and how we ought to speak.

We assume—in contrast to "Anglo-American empiricism"—that the limits of language are the limits of the world. Since all "meaning," intelligibility, identification, description, etc. depend on linguistic conventions, the demand to isolate a "domain" or "realm" of world, reality, etc., external to language asks for a conception of an actor/interpreter who is not originally oriented and who only acquires an orientation empirically. We assume that the type of actor required by this demand is impossible (inexplicable, incoherent) and, more frequently, that the capacity to imagine such an actor itself testifies to what *we* are arguing for. This is to say that the rejection of the assumption that "the limits of language are the limits of the world" can only occur as another confirmation of that relationship. That is, the relation can only be rejected *intelligibly*.[7]

De Saussure's Conception of the Sign

For de Saussure, the unit of analysis in the study of language is the sign that unites not a name to a thing but an "acoustic image" to a concept.[8] That the sign unites the signifier (sound-image) and the signified (concept) raises the question of how the sign itself is possible.

Since I mean by the sign the whole that results from the association of the signifier with the signified, I can simply say: *the linguistic sign is arbitrary*.[9]

This is important for linking de Saussure to Wittgenstein, for it suggests that meaning rests entirely upon conventions of agreement--that meaning (consciousness) is an accomplishment, a social product, that meaning has no "natural fitness" in and of itself.[10]

To say that the sign is a social product is to acknowledge its place in language, because we can now understand language as that complex configuration of practices—of human conventions and agreements—in terms of which we speak, i.e., signify. If we still cannot appreciate how language in this expanded sense is the limit of (and is) the life-world, perhaps it is because we do not distinguish properly between language (limits) and speech (between *langue* and *parole*).

Language . . . is not be confused with human speech. . . . It is both a social product of the faculty of speech and a collection of necessary conventions that have been adopted by a social body to permit individuals to exercise that faculty.[11]

To give language first place in the study of speech . . . (note that) . . . the faculty of articulating words—whether it is natural or not—is exercised only with the help of the instrument created by a collectivity and provided for its use: therefore, to say that language gives unity to speech is not fanciful.[12]

If we imagine the "speaking circuit" as the concrete speech act, we see that "execution is never carried out by the collectivity. Execution is always individual, and the individual is always its master. I shall call the executive side *speaking* (parole)."[13] Whereas execution is concrete and contingent, what is not contingent but necessary is for it to draw upon the resources of language; this need of execution (of speech) is not contingent but absolute.

> In separating language from speaking we are at the same time separating: 1) what is social from what is individual; and 2) what is essential from what is accessory and more or less accidental.[14]

Though language itself can be seen as an historical occurrence, its necessity resides in how it must (be seen to) provide for the intelligibility of the sign, or speech.

> Language is not a function of the speaker; it is a product that is passively assimilated by the individual. *It never requires premeditation and reflection enters in only for the purpose of classification....* Speaking, on the contrary, is an individual act. It is willful and intellectual. Within the act, we should distinguish between: 1) the combinations by which the speaker uses the language code for expressing his own thoughts; and 2) the psychophysical mechanism that allows him to exteriorize those combinations.[15]

Here, surprisingly, we get the mandate for a sociological conception of language that promises to ground the program on self-reflection. That language is "passively assimilated" by the individual and "never requires premeditation" reminds us of Husserl's conception of the life-world as a language in which (in terms of which) we live our life. Now, though, there is an opportunity to modify that life through "reflection." Theorizing as (self-) reflection—that is, speech's reflection upon itself or upon language as that representation of itself that is both greater than it and yet internal and necessary to it—is possible *given certain purposes*.

At this point, de Saussure leaves us with options that appear not to seek to "overthrow the existing state of things" but, rather, to direct themselves toward analyses of the ways in which language is *used* (to the way in which it occurs in speaking) and to its mechanisms of "exteriorization." In Husserl's terms, such purposes appear technological or descriptive, treating language technically (as if it were speech, *parole*). Nevertheless, de Saussure provides us with the opportunity to imagine another possibility for self-reflection: though we all share in the "passive assimilation" of language (of the life-world and its conventions and limitations), *in some cases and for some purposes we can require self-reflection as our mode of living in that world*. This is to say that in some particular cases and under some particular circumstances we can act under the auspices of the "deep need" for self-reflection.

Self-reflection upon the relationship of consciousness to life is not identical to consciousness as in "consciousness of this fact," because it is oriented by the "subjective interest" to "overthrow the existing state of things." In our terms, self-reflection reviews, reformulates, and recollects the relationship between consciousness and life not by being "conscious of this fact" (of this relationship) but by reconstructing or relaying the grounds of this relationship in the life-world. What this means in de Saussure's terms is that language reflects upon itself, it recollects itself in the form of speech's relaying of its own grounds in language. Thus, self-reflection is intelligible as the ideal discourse developed by consciousness about its relation to the life-world through its use of that very world. Self-reflection in this sense is language recollecting itself. Before directly examining this claim, however, certain of its resonances require development.

Sources of Order

The internal self-reflection of language upon itself could easily take the form of ascribing the orderliness and stability of language to sources (assumed to be) external to it. Again, in de Saussure's terminology, this would be to equate language with speech. The problem of order—of how knowledge is possible—now approached through the question of how language is possible, has led philosophers and practitioners in the various human sciences to either the empiricist supposition of a realm of prior objects or the rationalist posit of innate potentialities of mind and intuition.

> The study of language in its proper setting of human life ... led Wittgenstein into the philosophy of mind. For when he ceased to rely on a simple linkage between word and object, it was natural for him to turn to the users of language and ask what is contributed by them. A plausible answer is that something must go on in their minds. ... But Wittgenstein now argues that a word is not backed up by a single mental entity—for example, an image—which guides its application. The search for a unitary basis for the meaning of a word is not more successful in the mind than it was in the world outside the mind. Images need an interpretation ... even rules have to be interpreted. But perhaps it may be suggested that the intention of the person following the rule is the fixed point on which the explanation of

meaning [the possibility of language, of consciousness, of knowledge] can rest. However, according to Wittgenstein, even his intention is not a thing that exists self contained in the present moment leaving him no latitude in the future . . . there is always latitude since the pattern of human reactions is essentially flexible . . . it is impossible to eliminate these flexibilities. Even when the previous application of a word seems to dictate our reaction to a new set of cases, we still have a choice. There are always alternative ways of developing a series.[16]

Both rationalism and empiricism formulated an ideal language user as one whose accomplishment of consciousness (of language) was construed as a series of methodical connections between some foundation assumed as "self-contained" and various behavioral consequences. Such an actor was necessarily depicted as *compelled* by these constraints, and so a view of the constructive work entering into his action was suppressed. The fact that such an actor would even be depicted as a rule follower shows that *that* is not the criterion of adequate self-reflection, because the subjective interest of such a rule follower is still concealed even if we attribute intention to him, or purpose, value, and the like. The point is that all such formulations succumb to the itch to generalize and, thus, tend to conceal the conventional, oriented, and decisive character of the action. What is presupposed and yet treated as inessential in such attempts is a conception of the motivated character of action.[17]

Wittgenstein says that those who speak of such "simple matters" as these (objects, mind, intention, even rules) " . . . are merely noting a convention."

But what if I reply: To the *depth* that we see in [such simple matters] . . . there corresponds the *deep* need for convention.[18]

Wittgenstein's remark points out how action described in terms of generalizations about regularities is itself accomplished through a simplification in which we (the analyst, the describer) suppress the sense of the variety of different ways in which the action can be done as a sense that is essential to its doing. In this way, he reminds us that our preservation of the oriented character of the accomplishment of consciousness can itself only be accomplished by our respecting the social production and accomplishment of our own formulation. It is in this sense that we share with, and participate in, the life-world of those whom we describe.

But the implications of Wittgenstein's reminder appear disastrous, for they suggest that our only certainty—our only foundation—is "the deep need for the convention." Is this what de Saussure's "language" comes to? If the life-world ultimately refers to our "deep need for the convention," and if such needs differ from person to person, it appears as if the roots of language in life are essentially irrational and contingent, based as they are only upon the conventions of agreement. This appears to destroy the recognition of both Husserl and de Saussure of the socially shared and "trans-individual" character of the life-world (of language). Wittgenstein's re-formulation of the critique as a self-reflection upon language threatens to dissolve in a particularity so concrete as to render it unapproachable to the very speech that it intends to ground. The critique promises to liquidate itself by dissolving in "subjectivity," nihilism, or silence.

If our deep need is for agreement, then that need itself and the agreement(s) in which *it* issues are tied inextricably to particular circum-stances. The congeries of such circumstances—inaccessible to general description (indeed, to *any* description)—are Wittgenstein's version of the life-world and of its roots in the particular circumstantiality of our "need for agreement." When we are certain, he says, it is just that doubt comes to an end, that we agree to stop doubting. Why? *Because this is the way we speak.*

Argument

In answer to the charge that the intent to preserve the "subjective interest" of the actor dissolves in the subjectivity of reflection, *we* said that this charge results from an inadequate conception of the life-world, from a failure to understand the life-world as language. Now it appears as if our attempt to develop such a formulation actually strengthens the force of the objection. That is, if we have shown that the 'world' is the intelligible world and that intelligibility is a social product, and if the roots of intelligibility appear to be nothing other than "particular circumstances" that underlie conventions and agreements, we must work in support of a number of arguments.

(1) We must show how "particular" is not equivalent to "private" or "personal" experience and so does not necessarily reference ineffability, because it points to something common.[19] (2) We must show that to which it points is the topic *and* the source for the self-reflection of language upon itself (of speech upon language), whereas it is only the source (and not the topic) of speech's reflection upon its practices.[20] (3) We must show how this enables us to say that self-reflection does something more than "note a deep convention," and so, (4) we must begin to establish the distinction between the theorist and the member as a distinction that is rational rather than conventional, even though it occurs as a result of a "deep need for a

convention." (5) Finally, we must provide an argument for the supposition that some conventional needs are better (more rational) than others and hence that some "deep needs" are good and not just arbitrary.[21] Because these tasks are complex and mutually influence and interact upon one another, we will try to discuss points 1 and 2 in the next two sections.

NOTES

1. F. Jameson, *The Prison House of Language: A Critical Account of Structuralism and Russian Formalism* (Princeton, N.J.: Princeton University Press, 1977), p.23.

The vice of Anglo-American Empiricism lies indeed in its stubborn will to isolate the object in question from everything else, whether it be a material thing, an 'event' in Wittgenstein's sense, a word, a sentence, or a 'meaning.'

2. L. Wittgenstein, *Tractatus Logico-Philosophicus* (London, 1961), 4.12–12.

Sentences can represent the whole of reality, but they cannot represent what they must have in common with reality in order to be able to represent it—the logical form. To be able to represent the logical form we would have to be able to put ourselves with the propositions outside logic, that is outside the world. Sentences cannot represent the logical form: this mirrors itself in the sentences. That which mirrors itself in language, language itself cannot represent. That which expresses *itself* in language, we cannot express by language. The sentence shows the logical form of reality. It exhibits it . . . what can be shown cannot be said.

3. G.J. Warnock, *English Philosophy Since 1900* (Oxford: Oxford University Press, 1958), p. 58.

Is it necessary here to add that Wittgenstein of course does not suggest that philosophical problems are all 'about language'? Of course they are not; they are about knowledge, memory, truth, space and time, perception and innumerable other things. What he suggests is that, though thus not *about* language, they spring *from* language; as to the uses of language; they are to be solved . . . by coming to see and to employ our language properly. It would make no difference of substance here if one referred, instead of to 'language,' to 'concepts.' This may sound more important; but the problems were never thought to be trivial.

4. Cavell, op. cit., pp. 19–20.
5. P. Winch, *The Idea of a Social Science and Its Relation to Philosophy* (London: Routledge & Kegan Paul, 1958), pp. 11–12.

To ask whether reality is intelligible is to ask about the relation between thought and reality. In considering the nature of thought one is led also to consider the nature of language. Inseparably bound up with the question of whether reality is intelligible, therefore, is the question of how language is connected with reality, of what it is to *say* something.

6. Ibid., p. 15.

We cannot say then, . . . that the problems of philosophy arise out of language *rather than* out of the world, because in discussing the language philosophically we are in fact discussing what counts as belonging to the world. Our idea of what belongs to the realm of reality is given for us in the language that we use.

7. See H.G. Gadamer, *Philosophical Hermeneutics* (Berkeley: University of California Press), 1976, pp.35–36.

This by no means suggests . . . that the linguistically articulated consciousness claims to determine the material-being of life practice. It only suggests that there is no societal reality, with all its concrete forces, that does not bring itself to representation in a consciousness that is linguistically articulated. Reality does not happen 'behind the back of language'; it happens rather behind the backs of those who live in the subjective opinion that they have understood 'the world' (or can no longer understand it); that is, reality happens precisely *within* language.

8. F. de Saussure, *Course In General Linguistics* (London: Fontana/Collins, 1974), p. 66.

9. Ibid., p. 67.

10. Cf. Jameson, op. cit., p. 30.

11. de Saussure, op. cit., p. 9.

12. Ibid., p. 11.

13. Ibid., p. 13.

14. Ibid., p. 14.

15. Ibid., p. 14.

16. D. Pears, "Wittgenstein and Austin" in *British Analytic Philosophy*, eds. B. Williams and A. Montefoire (London: Routledge & Kegan Paul, 1966), pp. 35–36.

17. "Motivated character" refers to the necessary work done by any typification to exclude other senses and is always shown in *wanting* to speak in the way one speaks.

18. L. Wittgenstein, *Remarks on the Foundations of Mathematics*, trans. G.E.M. Anscombe (Cambridge, Mass.: MIT Press, 1977), p. 23e.

19. That ends are enforceably and intelligibly whatever they are taken to be, so that what is shared is a "deep need" for limitation; that the inability to fix a normal use for this common good does not deny its intelligible contestability as a conversational topic. See L. Strauss, *Natural Right and History* (Chicago: University of Chicago Press, 1953).

20. That such ends are the topic *and* resource for self-reflection because language is its topic and resource.

21. That the "deep need" for the convention of self-reflection is a need that is good, even though not all members of the species would agree.

Self-Reflection I:
Speech and Language

We have said that self-reflection upon consciousness and its relationship to the life-world can be represented in terms of the ideal discourse of consciousness reflecting upon itself. Self-reflection is intelligible as the ideal discourse developed by consciousness about its relationship to the life-world through its use of the resources of that very life-world. Now we see that "life-world" is a metaphor for language; but if consciousness is essentially implicated in the life-world, we know that it does not stand to the life-world as one of two parties to a dualism. Rather, reflection upon this relationship is a way of referring to speech's interest in recollecting language, where that very recollection occurs as an accomplishment of language. Self-reflection is speech reflecting upon itself—upon its roots in language—and so, since speech is only empowered to reflect *because* of these roots in language, we say that it is language that is recollecting itself. Similarly, the self upon which consciousness reflects is its place (the place of speech) within language. What is subject for this reflection would be itself (its own possibility). One point we can take up in this section concerns the question of how this "possibility" is made available as a topic.

Speech and Language

Following de Saussure, we say that language reflects upon itself insofar as we understand speech as reflecting upon its source(s) in language. Speech's governance by language means that when speech examines itself, it examines language: Yet, language is other to speech in the very same sense, for the reduction of language to speech or of speech to language obliterates the analytic distinction between speaking practices as concrete occurrences and language as their source or ground. We need to clarify the essential connectedness and difference of speech and language.

De Saussure's idiom is important here if we read it properly.

> The study of speech is then, two-fold: its basic part—having as its object language, which is purely social and independent of the individual—is exclusively psychological:[1] its secondary part—which has as its object the individual side of speech i.e., speaking . . . is psychophysical.[2]
> Doubtless the two objects are closely connected, each depending on the other: language is necessary if speaking is to be intelligible and produce all its effects: but speaking is necessary for the establishment of language, and historically its actuality always comes first. How would a speaker take it upon himself to associate an idea with a word image if he had not first come across the association in an act of speaking?[3]

These two "parts" that speech *has* are analytic parts. That is, these are two ways of reflecting upon the idea of speech as an intelligible and distinctive idea. On the one hand, basic to speech is the essential element of language, which makes reference to the sociality of the order of language as a normative order to which the action of speaking *must be* (seen as) oriented in its particular occurrence. Language is necessary insofar as the concrete action of speaking is seen as intelligible in "all its effects."

Language stands to speech as unity or a limit relates to multiplicity, and yet it is through the multiplicity of different speaking practices that language itself becomes available as what it is, as such an essential limit or unity. The other 'part' of reflection is the variety of speeches that embody in many forms and executions their source and ground in language.

> Language exists in each individual, yet is common to all. Nor is it affected by the will of the depositaries . . . speaking . . . is the sum of what people say and includes: a) individual combinations that depend on the will of the speakers, and b) equally willful . . . acts that are necessary for the execution of these combinations . . . (it) . . . is not a collective instrument; its manifestations are individual and momentary. In speaking there is only the sum of particular acts. . .[4]

Whatness and Thatness

De Saussure's distinction between language and speech hinges in part upon their different modes of existence. We might cite Heidegger's work to advance the suggestion that these different modes correspond to the distinction between possibility and actuality or between whatness and thatness.[5]

If actuality is the "completed product of an activity,"[6] that which *is* without respect to whether it "exists" (the essent, quidditas) names that which an existing thing can be: that which makes it possible as such a thing (possibility).[7] Any thing that is, is divided into its whatness and thatness. Whereas essence answers the question of *what* is a thing—what must it be if it is to exist in the way that it does—existence says of a thing *that* it is

(in) thatness, in which nothing seems to be said . . . about 'what' . . . essence is assumed as self-evident.[8]

We recognize this distinction from the *Meno*, where Socrates is asked a number of questions about virtue (whether it is acquired by teaching or practice or in some other way), and he asks in response, "How can I investigate the *that* of any thing if I do not know the *what*?" He then proceeds to instruct Meno on the difference.

As a start, we might suggest that in de Saussure's vocabulary, we can hear his version of the relation of language to speech as a way of making reference to the relationship between the whatness of speaking and its thatness. Although this is still a simplification, it begins to anchor us correctly.[9] Perhaps we need to imagine self-reflection in terms of the image of an ideal language user, who reflects upon his usage—his speaking—under the auspices of a "subjective interest" in recollecting his self (his language) as the essential limitation upon his speech. A philosopher has formulated the problem for such an actor as follows:

What must the conceptualizing observer of animal movements see in and around those movements that will license him to characterize the movements in a certain way e.g., as tying shoes?[10]

We understand this actor (this "conceptualizing observer" of the relationship of speech to language) as guided by some notion of necessity (of what he must see) that is neither self-evident nor inductively available for inspection. That is, his orientation includes his sense of decisiveness and of inessentiality, his motivated compliance to some notion of whatness that allows him to select and disregard. That it is this notion of whatness that prefigures and collects the "movements" *that* occur means that the historical precedent of speaking—the *fact* that movements occur—is only a concrete (though necessary) precedent when considered against the background of his image of whatness.

Those conditions will come out as implications of the observer's report.[11]

The conditions that he collects as responses to his sense of the (essent, whatness) intelligibility of what occurs are not the automatic products of the "movement" he sees, because he is endowed with the need to see "in and around those movements" what they mean. This is to say that because he begins necessarily as an oriented actor, a generalization of what he sees will not reproduce the conditions that he recollects. Similarly, it is misleading to say that his "concept" of the essent—of *what* he must see—determines those conditions, because the essent is not such a simple foundation, and the fact that he is oriented does not mean that he *has* an image of the essent in mind. It is not the essent that is deep: It is his need for some sense of decisive limit (of a sense of whatness) that is deep, and to this need there corresponds nothing but particular circumstances.

As Meno asked Socrates, if we already know the essent, why are we acting as if we do not know; why do we search for it? On the other hand, if we do not know the essent, how will we recognize it when we find it?

What this self-reflective actor knows is that he has a deep need for the essent: It is at the point of this need that whatness and thatness converge in the indeterminant and yet intelligible practices of language, in the speaker's recognition *that* he has a need for whatness. At the root of this enterprise is neither whatness or thatness, essent or object, but his recognition in that which occurs—as speech—of a deep need for a sense of its whatness as its limit in language. This deep need appears to him not in the form of an essent but in the *demand* that language makes upon him to recollect its limits through his examination of usage, of speech. To the actor, this demand crystallizes as the history of possible and actual usages, which is a conversation, where the power of that conversation makes reference to the way in which language's need for its own collectibility persists throughout any particular circumstances of success or failure.

Immediacy and Inaccessibility

A reflection upon consciousness (and its relationship to the life-world) can be treated as a very personal thing if one is doing it upon oneself, and a very enigmatic thing if one is doing it upon another. Perhaps it is seen in some sense as "psychological."

In our terms, to see a reflection upon consciousness as "psychological" would be a mistake. As we are using reflection, or self-reflection, such work is intended to capture the way in which consciousness reviews or recollects the *analytic* conditions deemed necessary for its intelligibility. Consciousness does not describe an empirical terrain or behavior, because the idea of its "occurrence" suggests its intellectual constitution—the way in which it is put together or collected as an intelligible distinction. In this sense, the particular circumstances of the occurrence or location of consciousness—whether it resides in oneself or in the other person—is inessential, because however it occurs and wherever it resides, there must be a constant standard of intelligibility presupposed for *it*.

Thus, the ascription of "subjective meaning" to consciousness is an analytic stipulation that risks specifying the grammar of consciousness: The particularity and circumstantiality of consciousness exemplifies such a stipulation rather than designates how and where consciousness occurs.

Consciousness as we have discussed it is a course of action, an accomplishment or social product. We have said that its sources are in life or in the life-world.

The source(s) of consciousness in the life-world refers to its source(s) in language. It is language that gives us (perhaps in particular circumstances) the power to produce (accomplish) consciousness as an intelligible distinction, which itself draws its own limits by constituting itself as what it is vis-à-vis what it is unlike. It is in this sense that the power of language is social, and it is in this way that consciousness is a social product; it is an accomplishment of language. Although our uses of consciousness are particular and circumstantial, de Saussure tells us that language is trans-individual, that it is social.

Following this argument, we might ask how reflection can be a very personal or enigmatic process if it is empowered by the social or by language. How can the life-world (language) be personal or private if the very idea of such a world testifies to the constraint of language, to the public character of language?

Apparently what the objection has in mind is that there is something to which language refers to which it is not adequate (as if the particularity of the world makes speaking about the mind of oneself or of the other difficult). But then we are only saying that it is difficult to *use* language on such occasions, a point easily conceded without attributing this difficulty to the "subjectivity" of, for example, the other's mind. If language enables us to put into words *and* to be unable to put into words, our inarticulateness is guided by language and not by the "material" about which language seeks to speak. So, we might ask if the "ineffable" or the "inaccessible" is a result of its distance (its privacy and insularity) or of our inability? And if we ask this, we can further ask: By what is our inability given?

Wittgenstein would say that in such a case what we call inaccessible (our feeling of inarticulateness) is our way of making reference to our being in doubt about what to say, that we cannot agree upon what to say (for a variety of reasons; perhaps too much or too little is imaginable). If our speechlessness is given neither by the inaccessible object nor by the technically paralyzed faculty of mind, it must be linked to our conventions for deciding upon what we can say in any particular case.

If we imagine the accomplishment of consciousness as an oriented and motivated display of subjective interest, our effort to describe the ways in which that interested action becomes constituted as "meaning," "intelligibility," "knowledge," and so forth depends upon our seeing some association or similarity in the links that constitute the action.[12] Wittgenstein says that what we see here as *deep* acquires its depth because of our deep need for the convention. What we need is a convention or a way of coming to an agreement about what we see (in this case, the depth of what we see). What is really deep, he says, is our human need for agreement.[13]

Because our speech depends upon (language, the life-world) the "deep need for a convention," which itself always depends upon particular circumstances, does this mean that such circumstances are ineffable or that such dependency is unintelligible? If the ineffable or the unintelligible refers to our inability to speak, is that question not settled by its own particular circumstances? In other words, before we address the heart of the objection we have been unraveling in its strongest form (i.e., the charge of the conventionality of self-reflection), we need first to show how the charge of subjectivity presupposes that what is particular is ineffable in a way that concedes what it denies, viz., that calling something ineffable rests upon "a deep need" for a convention, and that the recognition of such a deep need occurs as an instance of language, of intelligibility.

In such a way, we might understand the depth of the action (of its accomplishment), as its foundation or "deep structure," and we might attribute such depth to the particular character of the actor (the agent) that differentiates him from any other. The deepest matter in such a case could be his mind, his intention, his subjective interest, or his point of view. But we *feel* such matters are deep because such a feeling is agreed upon as a deep part or need of our life. After requiring him to be so oriented (after stipulating that *what* he is is oriented) we identify as deep (and possibly as inaccessible and ineffable) just what *that* particular orientation is. While we do have a "deep need" for that convention—the convention that requires us to say of him that what he is is oriented—whether or not we do treat as similarly deep what *that* orientation in the particular case is, is a question that is discussable.

It is because *we* are users of language that we can imagine and disregard other ways of saying what is to be said (that we can agree on a normal use, that we can be paralyzed by the multiplicity of different uses that would undermine the normal use). When we say that the experience of music cannot be put into words, are we saying something about music or about "putting into words"? To this we might answer: Both; we are saying something about the part music plays in our lives.

One feature of the power of language is that it promises a collectibility of its many signs as that which may intelligibly not be agreed upon. If we use "music" in this way, we are collecting in a particular case (music) our "deep need" of a convention for resisting the promise of collectibility as a feature of its very promise.[14] Is music ineffable, a private experience, subjective? Or are these ways of talking about how we deeply need music and use it in our life (in our language)? Can we still converse rationally about music, or is our inability to fix its "normal use" an invitation to retire? Is not the cornerstone of our tradition (the tradition of the Greeks) founded on the idea of the accessibility of even the "abnormal case" to conversation as a belief—as a deep convention—that we all need? Are we not founded on the idea that there is a reasonable way to respond to the unreasonable?

If is often said that music is ineffable. Now we understand what that means in terms of our notion of the self-reflective actor as a language user. He cannot see "in and around those movements" that constitute the life of music in speech what he *must* see as the "conditions" that fix its use as a normal case. He is in doubt about what to say, a doubt that is a conjoint result of his deep need for the normal case and of the particular circumstances that make the relationship between the possibility and actuality of this normal case essentially problematic. If the circumstances of our life—our language—make such a relationship essentially problematic for every sign, in some cases our need to agree allows us to create a normalization with assurance.

What might seem ineffable to the self-reflective actor results from his sense of inarticulateness at not being able to agree upon how to establish his "deep need" for a convention as itself a normal case whose possibility and actuality coincide.

Thus, the objection to the so-called subjective implications of our ascription of subjective interest to the actor and to the action appears to confuse a parameter (a necessary conceptual or grammatical condition for the intelligibility of the speech/action) with its description or empirical designation. To say that the action is oriented is to say we know that *what* it is is oriented rather than we know *that* it is oriented (and it is certainly not to say that we "have" the other's orientation or whatness, or that we can observe or see his orientation).

To know that *what* the action is is oriented, is to know its whatness, but it is not to declare that it is oriented in a particular way (that it exists as oriented in a particular way). Whether or not it exists as oriented in *that* particular way, *what* it must be is oriented. Subjective interest identifies what the action must be prior to and regardless of whether it is that in the particular case.

To say that speech depends upon particular circumstances is to say whether or not the fact that it occurs in the way it does, depends upon such circumstances (*that* it occurs is so dependent). But whether or not speech occurs in that particular way, for it to occur at all presupposes *what* it is.

Given what we have said up to now, why should the other's consciousness be claimed, as it often is, to be more enigmatic to us than our own? Is it that we cannot know the other's mind because he is distant, whereas our own mind is close to us? Now we can understand that this "enigma" is an accomplishment, that the difference between our mind and his mind loses its apparently essential character when we appreciate self-reflection as a reflection upon the language that we share.

If the enigma is seen as an accomplishment, it is then our convention that may not allow us to agree, and so we are more inarticulate—more doubtful—when it comes to his mind. That we are so inarticulate is given by our conventions rather than by our physical distance. It is our shared life-world that permits us to see a difference between my mind and his mind, the immediacy of mine and the inaccessibility of his.

This is not to deny that there might be a difference between the self-reflection upon one's own consciousness and the reflection upon the consciousness of the other. It is only to say that the difference is not given by the contrast between self and other in this way, but by the conventions in our (common) life-world, which permit me to feel assured here and in doubt there. In one sense—a very restricted sense—what is really other is neither his self nor my self but these conventions. We have called by the name "language" the conventions in terms of which any simple agreement ultimately reduces. If we forget this, we can easily begin to apply and use these very conventions as resources, and thus we could imagine the difference between him and me as essential. Of course, we cannot have his feelings or experience what he experiences, but that we cannot is settled by my particular use of a convention common to us both; it is not settled by the fact that I own my consciousness and he owns his.

Self and Other

The fact that knowledge is collected by language suggests that the difference between knowledge of self and knowledge of other is derivative upon, and grounded in, what they both share, in language.

The "social" is then not depicted by the difference between self and other—by the idea of *that* kind of relationship—but rather, by the conception of a relationship between speech and language. The primary social relationship is then between speech (as self) and language (as other), for it is this relation that provides for the intelligibility of any and all derivative differences and distinctions. Note in the following how Winch's attempt to sustain a derivative distinction between "two sets of relationships" actually confirms the way in which they are both (commonly) collected by language.

> Rules . . . rest on a social context of common activity. So, to understand the activities of an individual scientific investigator we must take account of two sets of relations: First his relation to the phenomena which we investigate; second, his relation to fellow scientists. Both of these are essential to the sense of saying that he is 'detecting regularities' or 'discovering uniformities'; but writers on scientific 'methodology' too often concentrate on the first and overlook the importance of the second. That they must belong to different types is evidenced in the following considerations. The

phenomena being investigated present themselves to the scientist as an *object* of study; he observes them and notices certain facts about them. But to say of the man that he does this presupposes that he already has a mode of communication in the use of which rules are already being observed. For to notice something is to identify relevant characteristics which means that the noticer must have some *concept* of such characteristics; this is possible only if he is able to use some symbol according to the rule which makes it refer to those characteristics. . . . Hence, the relation between N and his fellows, in virtue of which we say that N is following the same rule as they, cannot be simply a relation of observation: it cannot consist in the fact that N has noticed how his fellows behave and has decided to take that as a norm for his own behaviour. For this would presuppose that we could give some account of the notion of 'noticing how this fellow behaved' apart from the relation between N and his fellows which we are trying to specify; and that, as has been found, is untrue . . . because we agree in our reactions, it is possible for me to tell you something, and it is possible for you to teach me something.[15]

What Winch directs us to here is the recognition that any approach to the object is guided and prefigured by some normative conception of how to speak (in particular, about *this* object). That this "mode of communication" cannot be accounted for in terms of the kinds of observational statements that are intended to describe the inquirer's "relationship" to the object not only shows *its* difference as a relationship, but also shows that speech about the object must be grounded in some conception of adequate discourse (in a "mode of communication"). Yet, it is misleading to say that we are dealing with "two sets of relations," as Winch suggests, because the idea of "two" here (a relation to the object, a relation to one's fellows) obscures the fact that both relationships are instances of (are grounded in and made possible by) one normatively ordered sense of discursive adequacy that stipulates how to speak of the two in such cases. Winch's "mode of communication"— which collects both relationships because it is essential to their very possibility—is what we mean by language. His "mode of communication" is a way of referencing language, and thus what is essential is really the difference between speech *and* language (these "two" types) rather than the difference between one type of relationship and the other.[16]

Simmel's formulation of the rational inquirer as one engaged in a self-reflection upon the possibility of knowledge allows us to appreciate the force of this real (essential) difference. In discussing knowledge of other persons, he says the following:

Mutual knowledge [is] presupposed by every relationship. We are often not conscious of this because . . . we need to know only that quite typical tendencies and qualities are present on both sides.

One can never know an other person absolutely, which would involve knowledge of every single thought and mood.

One forms some personal unity . . . which . . . depends upon the portion of him which our standpoint permits us to see.[17]

We understand from this that parties to relationships presuppose knowledge of one another, i.e., they suppose knowledge prior to their contact. This means that they are oriented actors. Their knowledge is always and essentially *constructed*; knowledge must be given its form, it does not exist prior to human labor, for it is found neither in the world nor in the innate capacities of man. That such typical knowledge is constructed means that it is not neutral, because it is constituted according to social relevances that guide and motivate its accomplishment.

Simmel conceives of knowledge as acquiring its social character not through its realization as an "effect" of antecedent causes but because it is constructed just like any other social fact. The sociality of knowledge consists not in its causes or in its external sources but in its being an instance of the common, constructive, and ordinary activities of everyday life. Knowledge is then completely sociologized, for it is no longer segregated from the life-world as an external domain but is assimilated to the status of any social practice. Knowledge is then always and essentially—when viewed from the perspective of this tradition of sociology—an oriented social practice. This means that there is nothing other to knowledge because there is nothing other to the oriented social practices of membership. Self and other, accordingly, are not truly or essentially different, because each is part of common knowledge as common orientation.

Furthermore, because no principle is applied to distinguish types of knowledge—whether of God, other persons, or nature—the object loses its particular relevance as a way of distinguishing knowledge, and so what knowledge *is* is what is shared by all knowledges, and what it shares is that it is constructed. Everything true of knowledge of others should hold for knowledge of self or knowledge of geometry, when knowledge is understood as a product of constructive activity. And yet, if every practice is an instance of interactionally constructive activity (if every practice can be treated as such by the sociologist), it is difficult to imagine a limit upon knowledge and so to imagine a way of distinguishing knowledge from ignorance (or

knowledge from opinion), except through indefinite recourse to enforceable standards of interaction. When constructive activity is the source and limit of knowledge, where various interacting selves-others produce and sustain constructive activity, there is no other formulated as one that serves to frame and limit constructive activity except interaction. To locate the essence of knowledge in its constructive work tends to equate knowledge with interaction; it tends to dilute the idea of knowledge by treating its end or principled aim (its *agathon*, or value) as that which cannot be seen in anything other than its intelligibility.

This reformulation squarely raises the problem of theory and practice, for if knowledge acquires its social character by being assimilated to the status of any constituted practice, the theorist has no grounds for differentiating his practice of self-reflection from any other practice, inasmuch as his notation of how knowledge is constructed is a notation that is similarly constructed. If the theorist differs from the member only by knowing and orienting to the constructive character of knowledge, what this amounts to is that the difference between theory and practice resides in the theorist's knowing (the essentially achieved and constructed character of speech) that of which the member is forgetful. That is, the difference resides in the theorist's emancipation from any commitment to a principled way of speaking *except* the principle that all principle is defeasible. Simmel's reformulation of knowledge then appears to complete the conventionalization of the problem, for self-reflection acquires its distinctive status only through its capacity to describe rules and conventions where the "deep need" to so describe has no principled character, because it is itself grounded in rules and conventions that have no essential value (that are done customarily or by habit).

That knowledge is constructed is now taken as its essence. Its whatness as what knowledge is is disregarded, because whatness is understood as making reference to "having absolute knowledge," which Simmel claims we can never possess, because all we can do is interact, and we know that knowledge from interaction is mutually constructed knowledge that is guided by the selfsame standards of interaction to which that knowledge makes reference. Consequently, whatness is transformed to stand for *the fact that* all knowledge is constructed.

Furthermore, it is through this interactional theory of reflection that accessibility of the other is no longer a fundamental issue, because for interaction, life is essentially perspectival. Regardless of what we can see of the other, we can always "form a personal unity . . . ". Since what we see is typical and approximate, we have to select, to disregard and to leave things out. *That* we construct is necessary—it is what limits us—but whatever it is that we see in any particular case is variable, contingent, and depends upon the particularity of circumstances, which are always achieved through constructive work.

What one sees or knows results from the particular interactional circumstances under which seeing is done. These interactions are limits. To say that one's standpoint depends upon the "overall relationship" is to say that it depends upon the particular limits of this relationship—that is, it depends upon actual history, and history collects the chance associations between circumstancs. The overall relationship is particular, it expresses a limit. One's orientation to an interest in the other is guided by the history that they share as the history of their interaction. The history is particular because it is constructed, and what is constructed is determined by chance through the particularity of countless interactions.

As compared to a relationship that is limited by particular interactions, one might imagine an absolute relationship.

> One can never know another person absolutely, which would involve knowledge of every single thought and mood.[18]

An absolute relationship appears impossible because it is abstract, because it depends upon being a witness to every thought and mood. The absolute relationship depicts one who can (is in position to) observe every thought and mood of the other. But this is absurd, since it involves being the other. Simmel says that one can never *be* the other and that construction (forming a "personal unity") is an accommodation to this. But this raises several problems.

How can the impossible be a failure if it is an essential limit? It is as if social man lives under the shadow of this failure, his constructive work being an unhappy adaptation to the limit. Forming a unity has no point or reason—no principle—aside from making the best of a bad situation, of a situation of imperfect information. Given this view, the symbolic inter-actionist program can at best "note a deep convention," the convention of naming, typifying, and accomplishing intelligible constructions as the basis for interacting. In other words, given this understanding of the limits, symbolic interaction must take as its topic the description of the accomplishment of intelligibility ("meaning") in and as social practice. What symbolic interaction can note at most is that life originates in constructive activity, and so it is animated by the principle that the best discursive form for inquiry is to be "conscious of this fact," of the fact that interaction is a way of referring to the limits of what can be done and what can be said about what can be done. Being conscious of this fact, and of the ways this fact takes form in the varieties of circumstantial interaction, is knowledge for symbolic interaction. Knowledge is constituted of, and limited by, perspectives for seeing.

Does Simmel's recommendation that one can never know or have absolute knowledge suggest that absolute knowledge is impossible? Apparently not, for its denial here does presuppose its thinkability, its topicality. The statement itself (that "one can never know . . . ") is absolute. Absolute knowledge of what one cannot know, then, is necessary for Simmel to establish what one can know. Simmel distinguishes between the theorist and the practical actor by attributing "absolute knowledge" as a limit of knowledge to the theorist. But upon what is this claim based if all knowledge is constructed? In other words, how is what is here known by the theorist (Simmel) not another invention or construction? Simmel might say that the difference between the theorist and the member is in knowing when to stop.

To what kind of standard of exactitude does this image of "absolute knowledge" make reference? While his description of the standard sounds empirical, we suspect it reflects the deep need for a convention. Simmel anchors his conception of absolute knowledge in an image that pictures what it would mean to have continuous (and accurate) observational access to "every single thought and mood," to everything in the other's mind. But does not such an image presuppose that such an access is thinkable, and if so, does his recognition of the *depth* of the picture not reflect his deep need for the picture? It seems here, then, that even Simmel's conception of the limits of absolute knowledge is grounded in socially oriented treatments and deep needs for convention that are enforceable and intelligible. In this move, what is truly other for Simmel must be the needs and conventions that animate his practices, not the picture of absolute otherness that is realized through his application of these practices. These needs force him to recognize the constructive character of life as the interactive limits of a variable though commonly intelligible perspective. He cannot imagine anything other than this creative principle.

Conventionality

It appears that the beginning of an answer to the rejoinder that we invented in the previous section to the idea of the essential subjectivity of self-reflection can be developed through the notion that the life-world is a metaphor for language and that language constitutes the limits of the world. Yet, while this argument can be sustained in such a way as to exempt us from the charge of random subjectivity by showing the necessarily public or normatively ordered character of speech (of interaction), it still raises a crucial problem that is even more decisive in its implication, the problem of conventionality: There is nothing other than convention because any principle employed in such a discrimination would itself be the application of a convention. This is to say, if self-reflection makes reference to language's interest in recollecting itself, and if that "self" now appears as an other for language only in the form of the "deep need" to equate the question of *what* it is with the question of its own grammar, its thatness, then self-reflection will ultimately be ruled by the same particular circumstances that determine (arbitrarily? conventionally?) how we agree to fix the normal case. Eventually, we will argue that this understanding of the problem overlooks the possibility of a dialectical examination of "deep needs" and hence of a critique of conventions.

If our reformulation of self-reflection as the speaker's reflection upon his shared language showed the incoherence of the charge of subjectivity, we accomplished this by arguing for the public and normatively ordered character of language as the limit of what is intelligible, and so as the limit of the world. Consequently, we denied that private and spontaneous wants, values, and intentions are primary—that what is unshareable or ineffable is primary—because that which is first for a language user must be something shared, it must be some "deep need" for a convention or an agreement. That we can discuss such "deep needs" shows that the question of the common good is intelligible and that the need for discussing it is a need that is rational, that is good. In a way, the best "deep need" is the need to discuss and assess our needs.

Yet, intelligent objections can now be raised. It might be said that our argument (indeed, any argument such as this) forces us to concede that convention and agreement—that particular circumstances—are first. Since human agreements and the circumstances in which they arise are results of chance; we have no rational grounds for doing what we do since what we do is ultimately conventional. At best, we can note "deep conventions," and yet this very interest reflects the "deep convention" that animates us and impels our curiosity.[19]

The implication of this rejoinder would be that the conversation upon self-reflection must ultimately reduce to a discussion of different conventions, where the format of this discussion and any proposed solutions reflect only other conventions. Because there could be no transconventional ground for any particular proposal on how to speak, the differences between proposals are ultimately arbitrary. The charge of "subjectivity" is now raised in a deeper way, because the circumstances that ground any convention appear to be so particular that, at best, they can only be noted by self-reflection as itself another convention. What is ineffable and inaccessible to self-reflection is any reason or ground that is more than a "deep need for a convention." Because self-reflection must always be incomplete, it must always mask its origins from itself.[20]

Our examination of this problem raises a consideration of the difference between speaking and speaking about speaking. This difference is not given by the "object," as if in one case we speak about speech and in the other we speak about other things, because speech can be spoken about technologically or calculatively (think of linguistics), and speech about other things can be treated *as if* it is speaking about speaking (for example, as if it speaks about how we ought to speak).[21]

If the self-reflective actor is a language user, and if language is (as we have said) social, there is no essential difference in that respect between self-reflection and anything else. This is to say that because language use collects both self-reflection and common sense—both knowledge and ignorance—the difference between self-reflection as theorizing and self-reflection as practical reasoning cannot be drawn *there*.[22] If we cannot recognize self-reflection on the basis of what it speaks about, or in terms of the material it uses or the images that guide it, nevertheless we can—following Wittgenstein—still recognize self-reflection in terms of its particular circumstances, its particular "deep need."

It might be said that particularity assimilates self-reflection to the status of any need or convention within society. This is partially true and partially false. Self-reflection does occur as an interested and oriented need on the part of societal members, and in this sense its impulse reflects the need (shared by all) for a convention or agreement. On the other hand, the need that self-reflection expresses has its own character and shows its own interest. In this way, the need for self-reflection can be understood as both the same as, and different from, other human needs.

Like any action, self-reflection occurs in the life-world as an action in that world, as a move within language. Self-reflection is a species of practical action. As any practical action, self-reflection is guided by subjective interest, is oriented to comply in a motivated way with an end or aim; as speech, self-reflection is directed by its interest—by its end or aim—to speak well about itself. Self-reflection seeks to speak well about its relationship to language: It is that form of practical action that seeks to recollect its ground in language.

If self-reflection is distinguished by its "deep need" for conventions that will allow it to speak well about the grounds of speech in language, it will always and necessarily be involved in a discussion concerning the adequacy—the rationality, the value— of these conventions and how they satisfy the need to speak strongly. Self-reflection can only be envisaged as the course of action typically followed by a rational actor. That this discussion can never be segregated from the life-world or the language in which it occurs does not mean that there is no difference between self-reflection and ordinary language use. Rather, self-reflection is, in Wittgenstein's sense, an eccentric reflection upon language conducted from within language itself.[23]

What the objection to theoretic self-reflection asks is this: If self-reflection is a species of practical language, how can its very activity of reflecting upon itself distinguish what it is from another practical action, if any such distinction only rests upon another convention? If the distinction is formulated as essential or innate in terms of some "simple," self-evident proposition, then—given our argument—it is impossible, because it rests upon an incoherent segregation of action from the life-world (from language) and, so, of the theorist from practice. If the distinction is formulated as conventional, then it is irrational, because we have no good reason for differentiating self-reflection from anything else except through recourse to habit, fiat, or conformity.[24]

Yet, if self-reflection upon the possibility of language is practical reasoning's attempt to recollect its source—the source of practice—in the life-world, then self-reflection is the mode of life that shows an *interest* in addressing its source or foundation (in language). Before we seek to discuss in detail the objection that such a mandate (for self-reflection) rests upon grounds that are ultimately conventional, we need to formulate self-reflection as a distinctive, socially oriented, and organized interest or need by envisaging its subjective interest, its course of action, its motivation, and its normative order (or rationality). In doing this, we will be identifying self-reflection as both similar to social action, by virtue of those conditions it shares with all practice, and as different, by virtue of its distinctive parameters, by virtue of *what* it is. The self-reflective actor in such a case must be a rational enquirer, but we have to understand the particular character and limits of this rationality.

Thus, our intention is to establish the place of the enterprise of self-reflection as a course of action with a distinctive end or excellence, *given* that the roots of self-reflection (like any practice) are in the life-world (in the language in which we live).[25]

NOTES

1. By 'psychological' we mean—is to be treated as oriented action.

2. By 'psychophysical' we mean—is to be treated technically.

3. F. de Saussure, *Course in General Linguistics* (London: Fontana/Collins, 1974), p. 180.

4. Ibid., p. 19.

5. M. Heidegger, *The End of Philosophy* (New York: Harper & Row, 1973).

6. Ibid., p. 1.

7. Ibid., p. 2.

8. Ibid., p. 11.

9. It is a simplification because it suggests that the essent rules the accomplishment of consciousness just as the object was construed to do previously. This overlooks the *analytic* character of the life-world (language) as the "deep need" for the limitation of an essent that makes reference to something more than the essent itself, i.e., to the "deep need."

10. D. Shwayder, *The Stratification of Behavior* (Atlantic Highlands, N.J.: Humanities Press, 1968), p. 130.

11. Ibid., p. 13.

12. Cf. Winch, *The Idea of a Social Science and Its Relation to* Philosophy (London: Routledge & Kegan Paul, 1958).

13. L. Wittgenstein, *Philosophical Investigations* (New York: Macmillan, 1953), p. 142, 56e.

14. *This* is what puzzled Augustine and, much later, Gilbert Ryle about fixing the (normal) use of "time."

15. Winch, op. cit., pp. 84–85.

16. The difference between these two conceptions of difference—between these two types of relationships—is parallel to Derrida's distinction between differance and difference, where differance refers to the relationship between language and speech, which collects and grounds difference. J. Derrida, *Speech and Phenomena* (Evanston, Ill.: Northwestern University Press, 1973).

17. K. Wolff, ed. *The Sociology of Georg Simmel* (Glencoe, Ill.: The Free Press, 1950), p. 308.

18. Ibid., p. 308.

19. We would say that this could be true only if we do not expose our conventions—our agreements—as our limits in the course of our oriented use of them.

20. This is the sense of the so-called infinite regress.

21. This is to remember how self-reflection originates in the life-world.

22. That the distinction between theory and practice is practical means that the question of excellence (theory) needs to be posed as part of our life (as a feature of our practices).

23. Eccentric because—contrary to ordinary language philosophy—it does not intend merely to recapitulate the "ways in which we speak."

24. Cf. Rosen's argument against ordinary language philosophy in *Nihilism*; also, Strauss's critique of "conventionalism" and "historicism."

25. Our intention to establish self-reflection as the work of speech's reflection upon its sources in language should not be confused with the attempts of sociology, linguistics, philosophy, and literary theory to conceptualize and describe language as a topic. Without exception, these studies tend to be technological and diachronic (in de Saussure's sense) in their interests. Thus, for examples of what our interest in language decidedly is not comparable to, the following typical works should be consulted: T. Luckmann, *The Sociology of Language* (Indianapolis: Bobbs-Merrill, 1975), sociology; N. Chomsky, *Language and Mind* (New York: Harcourt, Brace, 1968), linguistics; J. Bennett, *Linguistic Behavior* (New York: Cambridge University Press, 1976), philosophy; and G. Steiner, *After Babel* (New York: Oxford University Press, 1975), literary theory. Such studies are all concerned with exploring the *behavior* of language.

Self-Reflection II:
The Sociology of Knowledge

One consequence of our formulation of the problem of self-reflection as an actor's interest in recollecting the possibility of language is that the action of using language is essentially oriented and motivated in a way that includes the action of self-reflection itself.

One problem displayed in the objections we have reviewed is that they treat self-reflection as an attempt to view or to review *behavior*, and so as an attempt on the part of consciousness (speech) to develop a *description* of itself as a behavioral occurrence, i.e., as a self-report. In contrast, we have discussed self-reflection as the action of reflecting upon the possibility (the whatness) of the language in which speech is essentially implicated. Self-reflection reassesses the grammar of the speaking practice instead of attempting to describe how the practice occurs empirically as a result of concrete conditions. In other words, there is a difference between self-reflection and self-report.

When the arts and sciences reflect upon their work, they tend to describe their investigations through controlled reflections upon their behavior or methods; they tend to make reference to the behavior in terms of which their objects are actualized. In this sense, our conception of self-reflection differs from the practical reflective interests of the arts and sciences in its effort to pose the question of how the speech of the arts and sciences is possible as a grammatical rather than empirical question—that is, to ask after the analytic requirements of speech.

In contrast to so-called common sense, self-reflection seeks to recollect what is there treated as a self-evident source(s) of speech. From the perspective of a project on self-reflection, the techniques of practical reflection in both common sense and the sciences appear as species of common sense, as examples of speech's attempt to redescribe its own occurrence *as* speech.

In the form in which we propose it, self-reflection is practical action, but practical action that is guided by an interest in relaying the grounds of a practice. According to Heidegger, relaying the grounds is

> either putting a foundation under . . . or replacing one already laid by a new one. It is precisely the idea that it is a matter of providing a foundation for an edifice already constructed that must be avoided. Laying the foundation, rather, is the projection of the building plan itself in such a way as to indicate on what and how the structure will be grounded.[1]

Relaying the grounds begins with an existing edifice—the practice, the speech—for which it does not seek to provide a foundation, because the fact *that* the practice is actually existing testifies to its already having a foundation. Relaying attempts to reveal the source of the supports for this practice (perhaps by noting that "deep need for a convention" upon which it rests). Relaying the foundation permits the supportive force of the already existing and effective ground to become evident. It does not seek to provide an extension of the existing practice (e.g., with new information), nor does it intend to propose new grounds (e.g., as a replacement) for the future achievements and modifications of the practice. Rather, within the confines of the actually existing practice, it seeks to recollect the "deep need" to which the practice is assumed to answer.[2]

While relaying the grounds of the practice (in language) could be seen as a descriptive enterprise, no facts are proposed here, for we are interested in possibilities. What is sought is a "perspicuous representation" of the phenomenon in which the human agreements to which it is responsive are imagined. We can develop this conception by considering a conventional approach to the problem that is fairly typical of the sociology of knowledge.

Berger and Luckmann argue that the "sociology of knowledge must concern itself with everything that passes for "knowledge" in society,"[3] and in this assertion they display their understanding of the legacy of Durkheim and Weber.[4] The phrase that particularly discloses this intellectual debt is "passes for 'knowledge,' " which we take to mean "belief." Not every opinion and whimsical speculation ought to concern sociology, but only what "passes for knowledge *in society*." How does "in society" further determine the subject matter of the sociology of knowledge? "Knowledge" shows itself to be in *society* by virtue of the fact that it displays itself in action as a rule that guides that action. Thus, every belief or item of knowledge (for our purposes "belief" and "knowledge" can be used interchangeably here)—when and insofar as it enters into, and becomes a part of, the practical actor's deliberative process as a rule to which he is oriented (an order)—is a legitimate "concern" of sociological inquiry. How does a sociological observer know that a particular action is rule oriented? The sociologist must argue in this manner: I find a conception of the event to be senseless as action unless the action is oriented to, and ruled by, certain beliefs, and since beliefs can be otherwise, it must be ruled by a normative order that supplies it with its oriented character.

From their major premise about what ought to constitute the subject matter of the sociology of knowledge, Berger and Luckmann draw a particular conclusion. They say that as soon as one grants this major premise,

> . . . one realizes that the focus on intellectual history is ill-chosen, or rather, is ill-chosen if it becomes the central focus of the sociology of knowledge. Theoretical thought, "ideas," *Weltanschaaungen* are not that important in society. Although every society contains these phenomena, they are only part of the sum of what passes for "knowledge." Only a very limited group of people in any society engages in theorizing, in the business of "ideas," and the construction of *Weltanschaaungen*. But everyone in society participates in its "knowledge" in one way or another. Put differently, only a few are concerned with the theoretical interpretation of the world, but everybody lives in a world of some sort.[5]

We find these remarks confusing, because we cannot imagine what it means to say that "everybody lives in a world" but few make it their business to provide a "theoretical interpretation of the world." Can it mean that few orient to (interpret, understand, hold beliefs about, and know) the world, even though all "live" there? If this passage does mean that, then it acts as if the difference between the few (theory) and the many (practice) is a difference between whether action is oriented or not. For if an actor does not orient to the world, then "world" means nothing to that actor, and in no sense can it enter into his deliberations; consequently, "world" ought not to enter into the sociological formulation of the grounds of that particular action. If, by "everyone lives in the world" but few theorize, Berger and Luckmann mean that everyone orients to the world but few make it their business to scrutinize those beliefs, to explicate and formulate their beliefs, or even be aware that they hold certain beliefs, then, indeed, we are in agreement that all "live in the world," but few "theorize." In this sense, few reflect about the beliefs that make it possible for them to "live" and act in the world—that is, few engage in self-reflection. If this is what Berger and Luckmann mean by "theorizing"—and we conceive of no other intelligible sense of that word—then all the more reason to focus our attention upon self-reflection as the recollection of the limits upon those usages (ideas and beliefs) that circulate in a society but that rarely and with great difficulty emerge into the public forum. In this respect, theory and practice are united by their roots in language (the life-world), but only upon relaying their grounds as unity.

"Are you trying to say," an objector might ask, "that great theorists know no more than the 'common man'?"[6]

Of course we are not saying that, but we are saying that "theorists" distinguish themselves from the "common man" by this "mere trifle" (*smikro tini auto*[7])—not only do theorists hold beliefs about the world (not only are they rooted in the ordinary language of the life-world), but they also attempt to reflect upon these beliefs and examine them. They have a "deep need" to relay the grounds of such usages.

"But, if what you say is true," an interlocutor might object, 'the theorist' (the few) actually teaches the member (the many) nothing, for those who listen to and believe what the theorist says must already have believed it before they heard it from him; on the other hand, those who cannot imagine that what the theorist is saying is true cannot be convinced of it unless they change their practices, which means that they must already believe it and therefore need not be convinced."[8]

If teaching means handing over to the student something he does not possess *at all*, then the theorist does not teach the member anything. But there is a sense of "teaching" in which the theorist hands over to the member (student) what he is already in possession of, and this sense of the word would qualify the theorist as a teacher. Plato used the word *mathesis* to characterize the manner in which the theorist teaches. He said that *mathesis* was a grasping or receiving by the student himself of knowledge from within himself.[9] Thus, the student grasps by means of his own ability what already lies within him, and he receives from himself only what he was able to find by himself. This is not really so difficult to understand, nor is it as mysterious as it might at first sound.

Perhaps an example will suffice to elucidate the sense in which the theorist "teaches." If we heard someone speaking English, we would not hesitate to say that he knows English. And if we were asked to explain what we meant by "knows" in this particular case, we would say that "knows" means "knows the rules of how to make a sentence that is intelligible in

English." If we were asked how we knew that he knew the rules of English, we would say that his speech itself displays that it is guided by the rules of English grammar. What if we learned that this person is uneducated and does not even know the difference between a noun and a verb, but that he is intelligent and willing to learn and wants to be taught English grammar? In that case, we would try to provide a foundation for what he already—in some sense— knows. There is no paradox in asserting that there exists a sense of the word "teach" in which the teacher presupposes that the student knows what he will teach him. It is precisely to this sense of "teaching" that the Greek word *mathesis* and its English derivative "mathematics" correspond.

Let us now return our attention to the distinction between the theorist and the practical actor, between (borrowing from Berger and Luckmann) the "few" and the "many." In what other sense can we *sociologically* imagine the theorist as teacher, except insofar as he calls the member's attention to the beliefs underlying its practical activity? The theorist reflects upon (his own and others') usage to formulate the conditions (the rules, the principles) that authorize it. When the theorist reports the results of his inquiry, it often appears as if these results describe something other than human activity. Instead of these conditions being seen as a normative order to which *we* (theorist and member alike) subscribe when speaking, they are seen as rules of language that are abstracted from particular circumstances and needs. In this way, the theorist often appears (both to himself and to the member) to be disclosing something about a "reality" external to, and independent of, language.

When Berger and Luckmann exclude "theoretical thought" as a legitimate focus for the sociology of knowledge, because "only a very few are concerned with the theoretical interpretation of the world, but everyone lives in a world . . ," they are saying that we should not study language because few know language but everyone speaks; thus, we should study speech. "Few theorize" in the sense of having a "deep need" to recollect the grounds of their speech, but "everyone lives" in the sense of speaking in an oriented way. In contrast, our contention is that for theorizing (self-reflection) to be conceived as rational human activity, it must be formulated as a practical actor's "deep need" to provide an account, or logos, of speech. The difference between theory and practice is not that one theorizes and the other "lives in the world"; rather, theorizing is the mode of living in the world that requires itself to act under the auspices of the "deep need" to recollect these common grounds.

To Berger and Luckmann, the difference between theory and practice (the few and the many) can only be that the few have resources to do what the many do not; the few have the methods and procedures to do more than "live in the world," to theorize. Thus, self-reflection can only be formulated technically, in which the difference between the "few" and the "many" lies in methods.

Observation and Interpretation

The contrast between technological or calculative rationality and the attempt to relay grounds can be amplified by resurrecting the argument initiated by Max Weber's writing on observational and interpretive understanding and developed further through responses by Parsons and Schutz. In this exchange, we can begin to delineate self-reflection as the course of action that attempts to recollect versions of sociological theory and methods as formulative responses to the question of how sociological knowledge is possible.

Weber's distinction between the two types of understanding is relevant:

> Understanding may be of two kinds: the first is the direct observational understanding of the subjective meaning of a given act as such, including verbal utterances. We thus understand by *direct observation* in this sense, the meaning of the proposition $2 \times 2 = 4$ when we hear or read it. This is a case of the direct rational understanding of ideas. We also understand an outbreak of anger as manifested by facial expression, exclamation or irrational movements. This is direct observational understanding of irrational emotional reactions. We can understand in a similar observational way the action of a woodcutter or of somebody who reaches for a knob to shut a door or aims a gun at an animal. This is rational observational understanding of action.

> Understanding may, however, be another sort, namely explanatory understanding. Thus we understand in terms of *motive* the meaning an actor attached to the proposition twice two equals four, when he states it or writes it down, in that we understand what makes him do this at precisely this moment and in these circumstances.[10]

Weber is depicting the grammatical condition of *verstehen* (understanding) in that the distinction here is intended to suggest a way of differentiating and collecting two *uses* of the notion of "understanding." Weber is not telling us what occurs in the mind co-relative with the process of understanding; rather, he is proposing conditions for the use of the term.

To ask what understanding *is* is to ask what is behind its use (its utterance); these are the (necessary) conditions for its intelligible use. According to Wittgenstein, these "conditions" are always rooted in particular circumstances, and we would not deny this. We ask, instead: Given the particular circumstances that surround the use of "understanding," how must these circumstances be acted upon by the self-reflective actor in order to produce a rational conception of understanding? An answer would be a beginning attempt to relay the grounds or foundation of "understanding."

Wittgenstein suggests that the use of "I understand" cannot mean the same as its visible accompaniments, because such "movements" are only seen as relevant given some image of—some convention for imagining—their collectedness. Yet, it is also true that the use of the notion of understanding cannot describe the process occurring behind, or side by side with, the accompaniment. To make reference to such processes is not to relay the grounds of "understanding" but to seek intelligible (external) correlates for the notion, *given* the security and self-evidence of what it is assumed to mean.

Weber says that we have an "observational" and direct understanding of "the proposition $2 \times 2 = 4$." Parsons comments that at first sight it appears as if Weber is making reference

> to an atemporal world of meanings in abstraction from concrete motivation. But the form of distinction is quickly lost again when Weber includes under that same category (direct, observational) understanding of 'what he is doing' when we see a man chopping wood (or aiming a gun). The latter case certainly involves elements of concrete motivation—it is impossible to interpret the movements observed without reference to an end to which they are related as means.[11]

Parsons' argument is that Weber "missed the important distinction . . . " between "an atemporal world of meanings in abstraction from concrete motivations" displayed by the propositions "$2 \times 2 = 4$" and "aiming that gun at an animal," which it is "impossible to interpret . . . without reference to an end to which they [the bodily movements of taking aim] are related as means."[12] In other words, Parsons suggests that Weber obscured an important distinction by collecting the fact of "understanding" $2 \times 2 = 4$ with the fact of "understanding" what someone is doing when he aims. Further commenting on Weber's mistake, Parsons says that the "important distinction" is "between motivation as a real process in time and atemporal complexes of meanings as such."[13]

Parsons then says that Weber mistakenly treats as observational understanding both the understanding that grasps "atemporal complexes of meaning," such as $2 \times 2 = 4$, and that can be decided on purely logical grounds and the understanding of how a particular act is accomplished, such as woodcutting or aiming the gun. In contrast, we would say that Weber disregards *that* difference as inessential because he collects such apparent differences as similar examples of how "direct observational understanding" is used by a typical actor. Although these examples appear to refer to concretely different situations, in both cases *a similar convention decides how what is observed is to be treated.* Or, it is not the difference between $2 \times 2 = 4$ and woodcutting that is essential, but the difference between our treatment of them as self-evident and directly observable, in contrast to our treatment of them as problematic.

What is similar in these cases is the decision to treat observational understanding as direct. In these "different" cases, we collect them by treating them as observationally correct, i.e., as self-evident. What is essential is our decision or the convention upon which we rely to so treat them. Weber does not say that $2 \times 2 = 4$ is the same kind of action as woodcutting. Rather, he says that a condition for the treatment of understanding an action as directly and observationally intelligible is the presence of some convention for disregarding other ways in which the proposition could be taken or the action could be done. Weber is explicating the use of "understanding" in its direct, observational form. This is his way of seeking to re-lay the grounds of a *treatment* of action as self-evident. When the self-reflective actor as a language user is appreciated as the focus of Weber's distinction, we note that this actor is formulated as one who orients to certain conditions—who uses certain conventions—to accomplish a sense of the self-evidence (of the direct observational intelligibility) of what he understands.

Weber is not describing the accomplishment of $2 \times 2 = 4$ or of woodcutting as empirical actions, because his reflection is directed toward the conditions essential for *treating* any action as direct and observationally evident. Whereas Parsons would say that aiming and woodcutting cannot be understood as instances of "direct observational understanding," because such actions have to be placed in a context of meaning, Weber says that these actions can be *treated* as direct because directness resides in the life-world (the language, the treatment, the convention) and not in the object. Thus, Weber wants to re-lay the grounds of the *treatment* rather than to describe the accomplishment of the behavior.

In a similar vein, Schutz notes:

> Weber would say that I understand by direct observation the meaning of a man's behavior when we see him performing such acts as chopping wood, grasping a doorknob in order to shut the door, or aiming a rifle at an animal. These observed movements of the other person's body Weber cites as the substratum of observational understanding. However, it is obvious that they have *already* been understood and interpreted as soon as they are called "woodchopping," "knob grasping," or "taking aim." What if the man wielding the axe is not really chopping wood but merely appears to be doing so? What if the man holding the doorknob is not grasping in order to shut the door but is merely holding it steady in order to repair it? What if the hunter is not taking aim at all but is merely watching the animal through the telescopic sight on his rifle? Observational understanding of the other person's outward behavior is clearly not enough to settle these points. These are questions of subjective meaning and cannot be answered by watching someone's behavior, as Weber seems to think.[14]

This objection clearly misconstrues Weber's attempt to re-lay the grounds of *treating* something as an instance of direct observational understanding in the sense that Schutz sees Weber as using "direct observational understanding" as a resource to "settle" some descriptive claim. Instead of saying that observational understanding settles the issue, Weber is formulating what direct, observational understanding means as a convention of social action or as an accomplishment of language. (While such an actor must be seen as a rational inquirer, we will eventually have occasion to ask after the character and limits of his imputed rationality.)

Similarly, "explanatory understanding" is rooted in different conventions, e.g., in the need to understand the motive and meaning of the action. The distinction does not reside in the action itself (in the ontological borders between entities), but in the movement and direction of the understanding itself, which is impelled by the need to go beyond "direct observational understanding."

Thus, Weber provides us with one way to begin to understand the self-reflective turn in sociology as an attempt to re-lay grounds of practice, an attempt that has its source in the practical interest of the speaker, in his "deep need" to make his life-world (his language) problematic. If common sense depends upon "direct observational understanding," and if the sciences represent only technical modifications of this treatment (even when they distinguish between subject-object, fact-value, description-interpretation, etc.), sociological theory attempts to reflect upon the grounds of all such treatments as courses of action. In this sense, the goal of such self-reflective enterprise will always be to re-lay the grounds of social action in "motive" or "meaning."

> We understand in terms of motive the meaning an actor attaches to the proposition . . . in that we understand what makes him do this at precisely this moment and in precisely these circumstances. . . .[15]

We must gather ourselves together so as to hear this as a stipulation about language use. It sounds as if "motive" describes some specific behavior that occurs when an actor "attaches" meaning. If our task is to understand "what makes him do this at precisely this moment and in precisely these circumstances . . . " it seems as if such a task is impossible because of the inaccessibility of *that* question. Yet, if the problem of the accomplishment of "meaning" (of intelligibility, consciousness) looks impossible, it is only because we confuse our capacity to know "motive" (to see *what* it is "in and around those movements" that constitute it) with having a motive (with the movements *that* constitute "motive" regardless of *what* it is). Whether or not he might ("at precisely this moment and in precisely these circum-stances") attach the meaning he (the actor) does to the proposition, and for the same reason, is a question that still presupposes that we can imagine seeing, "in and around those movements," the conditions or grammatical requirements for the intelligible occurrence of "motive" (where "occurrence" is understood in terms of a notion's place in language). Regardless of what happens here, we have to presuppose imagining a rule that limits the notion of motive to be what it is.

Weber senses this when he says, "A motive is a complex of subjective meanings which seems to the actor himself or to the observer an adequate ground for the conduct in question."[16] That motive *is* "the subjective meaning which seems to the actor . . . an adequate ground" is presupposed as *what* motive is regardless of the form *that* it takes "at precisely this moment and in precisely these circumstances." The distinction that Weber makes here between actor and the observer conceals the fact that such an "adequate ground" is stipulated by the observer as an essential condition for the *use* of motive (as a way of formulating *what* motive is). And as the theorist or observer comes to recollect this ground, the ground itself does not belong to him but is instead a shared feature of the life that collects both theorist and practical actor—the life of their common language.

The actor is then the self-reflective observer who asks of his speech (his use of motive) what he has to see "in and around those movements" that will "license him to characterize it in a certain way," e.g., as "motive." The first and perhaps central condition the actor locates, according to Weber, is that the actor *has* to orient to it (to motive, to *what* it is) as an adequate ground for his conduct; he has to orient to its whatness. The actor "observes" his speech—the movement that characterizes the various uses of "motive" in his language—in order to recollect the order that gathers together these movements as an order that is normative (to which he orients) and that can be represented in his formulation of "conditions."

That the actor orients to this "meaning" as adequate grounds for his conduct is stipulated by the observer (now understood not as an observer of behavior but as one engaged in a self-reflection upon language) through, and by virtue of, his recollection of what is in question as a normal case. To do this work, *he* must oversee in an oriented way a variety of senses that language makes available as actual uses of "motive" in order to recollect its possible sense as *what* it could mean despite, and in respect to, its particular applications. Unlike Weber's suggestion here, *the* motive is not passed between observer and actor as if they were two parties to the dispute over whether or not *he* has it. Rather, subsumed in the observer's description of motive is the essential assumption that such an actor must orient to it as a parameter of *what* social action is, and thus the observer's interest is inextricably tied to the grammar of action as equally a grammar of observation.

It would be impossible to be observant except as observation is understood as action, for example, and so the observer is exercised to reacquaint himself with the need for action as the reason for observation. With motive, say, it is not who has it but how motive is conventionally necessary (or conventionally unnecessary) as a need of action and therefore a basis (or not) for some relation of the subject observed and the observing subject. No amount of technical apparatus alone can establish a relation outside this "understanding." Insofar as Weber's *verstehen* is addressed to the need for action, *verstehen* is necessary. Weber thus reviews understanding as a means of establishing the possibility of observation as the equivalent of the possibility of orientation, a possibility we suggest arises only by reflecting upon the whatness that is action. Weber's expression of observation-as-understanding returns us to the social production of consciousness, now seen as the kind of reflective work that intends to observe the whatness of action as the limit and genesis of inquiry. We would like to think that Weber can be seen to formulate observation *as* self-reflection by returning the observer to society. He does not draw the line *between* the observer and society, but around them, because both are oriented actions, as is anything social. The observer is an actor for Weber because the observer lives inescapably within language. To emancipate himself from language would be to forego the opportunity to inquire.

We would say here that Weber proposes a life-world of understanding as that which joins the observer to action in the social (re)production of consciousness. Oriented inquiry—what Weber calls adequacy—is not the correctness of the observer but rather his orientation to the need for understanding as the relation between observer and observed, just as it is the standard of adequacy among all social actions. Otherwise, he could not be observed to be observing, he could not be understood to be oriented to the idea of understanding. He could not, in other words, be oriented to inquiry except as he orients to himself as a course of social action.

In these respects, Weber helps to locate in a particular way the deep need of inquiry—what Marx needs as the real forces of inquiry, what de Saussure needs as the language that animates the speech of inquiry, what Wittgenstein needs as the form of life of inquiry: *causally adequate interrogations of . consciousness are those that treat consciousness as oriented action, and oriented action as sanctionably intelligible action.* What is common to the social relation of observer and observed is what is common to anything and everything social: the language of sanctionable intelligibility.

This is to say, as we formulate Weber, that the possibility of language is one that is worked out in the course of relations that are simultaneously sensible and sanctionable, a possibility within which observers themselves must inevitably participate (this is its necessity), regardless of particular or formal methods and techniques. Weber endows every actor and every action with a certain kind of self-reflective capacity: to orient to the need, expressed as social sanctionability for intelligible and committed *praxis*. All action and all actors are thus capable of theorizing (albeit in a specific way that we address further on) in that all action orients to its own potentially sanctionable nature. It is through this relation of orientation and sanction, now consciousness, that social structure, life-world, real factors, forms of life, and so forth are produced and accomplished according to our formulation of Weber's need.

Modes of Self-Reflection: Otherness in Symbolic Interaction and Ethnomethodology

At this point, we must realize that our concept of self-reflection as the need to recollect the grounds of speech in language does not entail one particular mode of theorizing because it is possible to treat recollection and sanction either technically (in terms of the socially enforceable grounds of "meaningful" practice) or (let us say) dialectically (in terms of the principled foundation of practice). This distinction corresponds to a difference between a focus upon rules and a focus upon principles, and it can only be developed by considering the two senses of rationality to which these foci correspond (and, ultimately, the different senses of the normative order upon which they each depend). We need now to examine the nature of sanction, we need to examine the "motive" of sanction for the self-reflective actor as the motive of one who acts under the auspices of *what* sanction *is*. To do so, we must be able at least to imagine that problems of social significance or principle are not identical to problems of social force or rule.

The contribution of Weber allows us to see that there is nothing Other to what is worked out and accomplished by actors in enforceably intelligible ways. This means that there is nothing Other than the oriented practices of membership, and so the stipulation raises the question of whether there is (for self-reflection) anything Other than opinion—whether absolute knowledge is possible.

Recall Simmel's comment that "one can never know the other absolutely." This means that one can never know what is different "absolutely." Because to Simmel knowing is inexplicably tied to enforceably intelligible social practices, this suggests that one can never have recourse to practices that will enforceably allow one to "know" in an unequivocal way. Apparently what Simmel means is that we are not in a position to "directly observe" every single thought and mood of that which is different from us. In other words, one can never be in such a position to know the Other directly because *one is not the Other*. The difference between one and the Other (between the self and the other) is absolute. And yet, the problem is roughly the same with oneself: while we might be in a position to know the self directly, Simmel tells us

> If we look closely at our conceptions as they pass our consciousness in a continuous temporal sequence, we find that there is a very great distance between any regulation by rational norms and the characteristics of these conceptions: namely, their flaring up, their zig zag motions, the chaotic whirling of images and ideas which objectively are entirely unrelated to one another, and are logically unjustifiable, only so-to-speak probative, connections. But we are only rarely conscious of this, because the accents of our interest lie merely on the 'usable' portion of our imaginative life.[17]

Our reflection— whether upon the self or the other—is fundamentally alienated. Simmel allows us to see that the difference between the self and the other does not surface in the differential accessibility of self or other to our reflection, and so he raises the problem of the status of the other. That is, if the other is that which we can never know directly, it cannot be the other person because *we can never know our self directly either.*

Note, though, that Simmel's remark that "we can never know directly . . . " is a declaration that is direct and absolute. *That* we can never know is, apparently, known absolutely by the inquirer. It seems that whether or not we can know absolutely and directly is given and made possible by our conventions for treating the world as direct and absolutely knowable. As in Weber's discussion of understanding, Simmel points to what we feel we need in order to treat something as direct and absolute: as a social practice, the treatment is first. That we can never know the other absolutely then says that our decision to treat the other as that which we can never know absolutely makes reference to an understanding that is absolute.

This decision points to a sociological conception of the other—of that to which we orient (that which we treat and relate to)—as being inaccessible to direct and absolute knowledge. It is a conception of the other that grounds the doctrines of sociology associated first with symbolic interactionism and, eventually, with ethnomethodology. That is, other is produced through social practice as that which is inaccessible to literal description. And because speech essentially glosses (we cannot speak directly), otherness is an omnirelevant and omnipresent feature of all speaking. Other is then represented in our discourse as the socially organized and enforceable sense of the limits of our speech.

Yet, Simmel tells us, in the face of such a limit—of such inaccessibility— we can and do work to "form some unity," some typification of that which is inaccessible. This is to say that the actor still has a descriptive interest in overcoming his perspectivality (his human limitation) in order to construct an approximation of the other. Inquiry is always conventional, an adaptation or convenience. In contrast to Simmel, Garfinkel maintains that we do not need to talk about the other in that way, as inaccessible, because otherness dissolves—for the sociologist—into the intelligible and enforceable oriented practices of membership. In other words, ethnomethodology develops the (more or less) primitive Simmelian recognition of otherness as its inaccessibility to literal description to the point where it is conceived as the multiplicity of dispersed and enforceable intelligible social practices generated and utilized resourcefully in the routine organization of social knowledge.

Ethnomethodology

It is this grasp that is expressed by interests in "everyday life" as a rubric for social inquiry. The standard for any speech, action, method—their measure—is the member of society conceived as one who is oriented to the intelligibility of action as a sanctionable affair. The nature and limit of consciousness is here re-formed as the nature and limit of the member:

> [Our] central recommendation is that the activities whereby members produce and manage settings of organized everyday affairs are identical with members' procedures for making those settings 'accountable.'[18]

What we can say about our affairs is identical with the ways we do them. Consequently, our limit is the limit of convention, because convention is what is enforced as accountable (as intelligible) in what we do. Our task as inquirers thus devolves around the understanding of inquiry as itself a convention:

> Wherever studies of practical action and practical reasoning are concerned, these consist of the following: (1) the unsatisfied programmatic distinction between and substitutability of objective (context-free) for indexical expressions; (2) the 'uninteresting' essential reflexivity of accounts of practical actions; and (3) the analyzability of actions-in-context as a practical accomplishment.[19]

We interpret Garfinkel's usage of 'wherever' to include whoever and whatever—he is recommending that practical reasoning is enforceable whether the inquiry is professional, sociological, commonsensical, basic, or applied. Otherwise, the "distinction between and substitutability of objective" (read scientistic) for indexical (read members') expressions would not be "unsatisfied," nor would the "uninteresting" reflexivity of practical accounts be treated ironically with regard to the social scientist. For ethnomethodology, observation is the form of life, in Wittgenstein's phrase, for inquiry into that selfsame form of life: convention. Social science is thus indexically tied to its materials, not by choice but by necessity:

> *Recognizable* sense, or facts, or methodic character, or impersonality, or objectivity of accounts are not independent of the socially organized occasions of their use. Their rational features *consist* of

what members do with, what they 'make of' the accounts in the socially organized actual occasions of their use.[20]

Garfinkel's solution to the problem of inquiry makes the resource for inquiry (observation) identical with the topic of inquiry (everyday life) by making the limit of language (and of sanction) equivalent to the limit of convention—there is no other way to speak except conventionally, enforceably, intelligibly. The production of an account is equivalent to the setting of that account, the observer equivalent to the member, because both are enclosed within the limit of convention. Inquiry becomes self-reflection in a very specific way; it becomes the self-reflection of the member. Whatever the difference between lay sociology and professional sociology, it is only technical and is not to be confused as an essential difference:

> Wherever studies of practical actions are involved, the distinction [between observer and member, resource and topic] . . . is always accomplished *only* for all practical purposes and attainments of sciences in and of the organized activities of everyday life . . . is an essential reflexivity.[21]

Thus, for example, while there may exist differences in technique between the sciences of everyday life and everyday life itself, these techniques are only given by convention. As such, the professional's equipment is intended only to bring him closer in understanding to the lay member, to convention. Difference, where it exists, exists to be overcome and not sustained, in the sense that all difference originates in, and is accomplished by, practice, by the same. Speech can vary, as in a dialogue, but only as a way of showing the common conventionality of the variants.

The dualism between objective observational methodology and subjective members' actions thus disappears in a way that makes any inquiry, whatever its source, indexically tied to the circumstance in which it occurs. The methodic or structural or intelligible observation is only possible insofar as it reproduces the methodic or structural or intelligible member's action. Members are reflective, oriented to the enforceable intelligibility of their own and other actions. They produce social structure as sets of conventions that develop and change in terms of these actions. The observer cannot therefore merely be an onlooker, but must orient to enforceable intelligibility as the only means for understanding the indexical social relation upon which his account will rest and from which it must be seen to spring. The observer studies society from within (language), and language is, for ethnomethodology, identical with the conventions that enable inquiry in the first place. Adequate sociological theorizing must formulate adequate members' theorizing, because the agency of each is language as convention. In this sense, the actor for ethnomethodology is convention; convention, being the simultaneous source and object of orientation, makes behavior methodic and thus serves as the agent of society and the agent of societal accounts, descriptions, and inquiries, wherever these may take place. Enforceable intelligibility is the convention by which every conventional practice must proceed. The origin of society is convention, conceived as enforced intelligibility. Objectivity, for instance, is to be discovered exclusively in whatever is enforceably intelligible, and thus is a constraint upon the usage of members, lay and professional. In this way, scientific standards of objectivity become just another form of potentially enforceable standards, and science becomes another form of practical reasoning, i.e., just another convention.

Whatever the practical topic—science, children's culture, economics— the resources, as limits upon what one might do with these topics, remain equally practical as sets of pervasive and methodically circumstantial particulars or conventions. Our deep need is here conceived as orientation *en vivo*. Every study is a participation, since practice is not just the object of inquiry but the very condition of its possibility. Because the notion of a "member" includes the social scientist, it is impossible for the latter to substitute objective expressions for the member's; or rather, to do so would be to fail to be oriented and thus to offer some unenforceable version, and hence to fail to know one's place as a conventional member of language.

The whatness of membership, then, is put forth as the resource and topic of inquiry, and we now need to examine membership as ethnomethodology's formulation of the limits of inquiry. That limit is in a continuous line with Simmel's conception of the other.

We have said that the other only *appears* to Simmel as that which is different and, so, as that whose otherness is contingent upon its *appearance*. To Garfinkel, other is the multiplicity of dispersed and enforceably intelligibile social practices that are indefinitely expandable possibilities integral to any usage. For Simmel, what appears as other acquires its status observationally (it varies "with the standpoint from which it is formed"). This conception of other, then, is an observer's conception: What is other is that which is not accessible to continuous, literal, direct observation. In contrast, Garfinkel generates a conception of the world in which everything is tied to enforceable and intelligible practices, a world in which there is nothing other than these practices. In such a world, the distinction between the theorist and the member dissolves except insofar as the theorist's is an interest in the accomplishment and social organization of such practices. Garfinkel then seeks to eradicate the type of difference to which "other" refers by treating other as a technical difference between the one whose practical interest is practice (the man on the street) and the one whose practical interest is the study of practice (sociologist, observer, scientist, et al.). Because—according to Garfinkel—all we need in order to talk are practices, we do not have the need to talk in the way Simmel does. Other does not refer to the inaccessible but to the indefinite and infinite expandability of speech. Garfinkel's notion of the "substitutability between objective and indexical expressions which is problematic in every particular case" is a way of making reference to the unlimited character of speech in this sense: that any limitation is internal to speech itself as a feature of its oriented and enforceable reachievement of its own sense on any and every occasion.

The sociological conception of other (whether in symbolic interaction or ethnomethodology) as that which is not accessible to direct and continuous observation or as the indefinite expandability of practical interests, is itself given by (is grounded in and made possible by) a "deep need" *to think in that way about other* (to think of its access as criterial for other). What gives this need to think in that way? The whatness in which this deep need is grounded cannot itself be supposed as the other for whom descriptive approximation is possible. At some point, constructive work must come to an end. In this form, sociology represents that "deep need" in the form of an imperative—a principle—recommending either that "one can never know" or the "unsatisfied programmatic distinction . . . between . . . objective (and) . . . indexical expressions." Yet, these principles are not the result of "direct observational understanding," and if they are achieved through enforceable practices, then intelligibility needs to be discussed as something more than "consciousness of this fact." That we deeply need to think of other in these ways is made possible by Other—not by the other we think of as inaccessible or as a feature of the indefinite expandability of speech—but by the Other that constitutes the particular circumstances of our language (our life-world), which makes its demand upon us.

In the work of Garfinkel, Simmel's imperative that "one can never know . . . absolutely" is transformed into an inaccessibility that is only accidental. Because of the indefinite expandability of usage, at any one moment, other is that which has not yet been described. The indefinite expandability of the interest in practical topics means that since anything could be a topic, whatever is not is waiting. Other is not the essentially unformulable, it is not yet formulated, and so it always refers to a technical or historical difference. Other *could* be formulated, and awaits the (accidental) chance.

Yet, within the context of the ethnomethodological project, the technical distinction between self and other becomes assimilatd to the technical difference between theorist (as one who has a "deep need" to make enforceable intelligibility a topic) and the member (as one who finds enforceable intelligibility "uninteresting").

Ethnomethodological principle is essentially historical: The reachievement of intelligibility always and necessarily displays some oriented exclusion in a situation of choice, an exclusion that recommends to the inquirer that the member needs in each and every situation a rule he can consult to reproduce the intelligibility of the interest that is ascribed to him as his problem. Because the ethnomethodological version of Simmel's absolute knowledge would be the comprehensive list that anticipates every contingency, what is impossible for ethnomethodology is an action that does not leave something out.

If Other cannot be the inaccessible, then it is that which makes the demand upon us, that which compels us to do as we must. Simmel and Garfinkel act out the demand of Other to think of Other in the ways in which they do. More, if this demand is truly Other, its alterity does not reside either in its inaccessibility to description or in its essentially irremediable character, but in the way it is necessarily implicated in our life (in our language) as a deep, necessary, and particular agreement.

Simmel says that what is other than constructive work is inaccessible. Garfinkel handles this by saying that inaccessibility is itself a feature of constructive work, suggesting in his turn that we do not need anything other than enforceable intelligibility. Other is then viewed ironically as the disinterest in enforceable intelligibility exhibited by the member.

Sociology recommends that other stands to self as if it is an opposite, thus, merely different in degree, not in kind. In contrast, we suggest that Other is the order that makes its demand upon the speaker to speak in the way he does about difference. True alterity refers to language and to the demand it makes upon speech. In this sense, Other is similar to a principle. When Simmel says that "we can never know . . . " he is showing us the principled way of discoursing about other. That principle does not reside in *what* he says about other (e.g., *that* "we can never know") but in how his speech brings attention to a principled way of discoursing (e.g., that one ought to focus upon the kind of distinction he makes between self and other, direct and indirect access, absolute and perspectival knowledge, and so forth).

Other as Normative Order

> Subjective attitudes constitute social action only so far as they are
> oriented to the behavior of others.[22]

Who are these "others"? Recalling our conception of how inquiry turns
"attention . . . to principles recommended for acceptance," we might ask to
whom the inquirer is seeking to appeal? It is only derivatively answered by
the notion of "other persons" or by the idea of the causal determination or
influence exerted by these persons upon action. Finally, it is not answered
by the idea of the member as one who finds constructive activity essentially
"uninteresting." According to Weber, social action requires that one orient
meaningfully to others,

> to certain determinant maxims or rules . . . such an order will be
> called 'valid' if the orientation of such maxims includes, no matter to
> what actual extent, the recognition that they are binding on the actor
> or . . . a desirable model for him to imitate.[23]

"Behavior of others" to which social action is oriented is a way of
referencing the actor's belief in the existence of a "legitimate order" as a
perceivedly binding (*because* it is valid) order to which he seeks to comply.
What is "other" to the social actor is only derivatively other persons, but
more essentially, the otherness of a perceivedly valid and binding order. In
this proposal, we have formulated such an order as language.

The orientation to the otherness of this order (of language) is meaningful
not only because the actor is aware of it and is *responsive* to its validity but
because its meaningfulness *consists* in its validity, and its validity is not
abstract but binding for and upon him.[24] This is because meaningful action
(discourse) takes account and orients in its course to the order of language
as a valid and binding order, i.e., to what the order demands. "Orientation"
makes reference not to a puerile "awareness" of the order, but to the mode
of taking into account the way in which the order takes into account, to the
way in which the order orders (the way the order hears and limits, demands
and calls). If meaningful social action is quintessentially discourse, the
valid and binding order to which it orients is language. It is language that is
Other to speech.

Social action is then ruled by the order in that it is guided (oriented to) by
the need to comply with the order. If we imagine the order along the lines of
the problem of the self-reflective actor, we can understand it as the (ideal)

hearer or auditor for his speech. In turning attention to a principled way of speaking, he says "this is how speech needs to be heard."

As he turns attention to a principled way of speaking, the self-reflective actor is not only critical (one who notes the conventionality of language), but also affirms and recommends principles of adequate discourse. And he does this despite and insofar as (his) speech is conventional, because he risks acting on the "deep need" to propose how we ought to speak. The difference between self-reflection as critical or technological and as affirmative depends upon the conception of Other, of the order. For self-reflection, the other does not materialize as the different—as the essentially inaccessible or the accessible-but-not-yet-formulable material, for example—because then the other appears only as a technical order of method, as instrumental rules for creating access to material. For self-reflection, the order rules and subjects as valid *within* the life-world; for technology, it *is* the rules that inquirers use to construct (access to the difference that is) subjects. Other does not limit in the way a condition can limit, since conditions are taken into account by virtue of the Desire to exemplify something other itself. Other is not that with which we establish a cognitive or interpretive relation and so it is not that which pertains to the achievement of evils but expresses the desire to address the quality of words in a way that supplies various interpretive relations to conditions with their rational character.

We have stipulated the self-reflective inquirer to be (1) a social actor and, so, (2) oriented in a subjective (meaningful, motivated) way (3) to a valid and binding order and (4) to have reformulated that order, first as the life-world, subsequently as language. In saying that the inquirer is ruled by the order, we do not suggest that it "determines" him causally but that its "validity" is the result of whatever particular circumstances have invited him to find it "meaningful," where these circumstances make reference to his needs in the life-world or language.

From our conception of the social actor as one who is an oriented user of language—one who discourses under the assumptions of our conception of social action—we can now begin to understand the order as equivalent to an auditor or hearer. Its validity is ideal in the sense that it is that to which the actor seeks to comply as a compliance that is needed and not just a compliance that is expected or enforced. That the actor orients to this order as an auditor means that it is not treated as if it were a passive listener but with respect. In other words, the actor needs to feel that he has heard (that he has himself audited) what the order demands. Consequently, when the inquirer turns "attention to principles" of adequate discourse recommended for acceptance, he is not speaking (in the deepest sense) to a particular audience, but is making reference to the way in which he has audited the demand or order of an ideal auditor. Such an ideal auditor has been referenced as community, tradition, and language. We say that every inquiry as a course of social action situates itself (by recommending or proposing *its* work) as a response to what it is as a valid demand, and so as an example of how to live under the terms of that demand.

Theorist and Member in Ethnomethodology

The concern with the "reflexive" character of practical action that distinguishes ethnomethodology as a theoretical project—as a program in self-reflection—is not a concern that *essentially* differentiates the theorist from the member; this difference is technical, since the member, too, has an opportunity to engage in self-reflection, *though as a matter of fact he does not in particular cases take up this challenge.* That the theorist is distinguished by this need means that he is interested where the member is not.

> For members to be 'interested' would consist of their undertaking to make the 'reflexive' character of practical actions observable . . . without thought for corrections or irony.[25]

Obviously, then, self-reflection undertakes to carry on such a project "without thought for corrections or irony." We suggest that Garfinkel's problematic use of "irony" here equates it with something like "invidious comparison," because a rational distinction between theory and practice (between speaking about language and speaking about speech) absolutely requires an ironic relationship between the inquirer and his usage (his materials).[26] In fact, Garfinkel's writings display a programmatic irony through and through.[27]

Garfinkel appears to have in mind Weber's remark that subjective meaning "in no case refer(s) to an objectively correct meaning or (to) one which is true in some metaphysical sense."[28]

To say that self-reflection undertakes the attempt to "make the reflexive character" of practical actions observable "without thought for corrections or irony" is to say that the project does not intend to realize itself in versions of the action that are stipulative proposals. Although the aim of ethnomethodology is fundamentally descriptive, Garfinkel should recognize the ironic character of description. Perhaps he means to say that a descriptive program that intends to be competitive with other descriptive research projects cannot survive if it dwells upon its ironic character. His interest is to make whatever is done observable as a description of the way it is done without respect to corrections or irony (i.e., without respect to principles or to the gap between speech and language). Where the theorist is distinterested in principles (correctives, irony), his analytic interest (which is precisely what members *happen* to be disinterested in) is in "making observable" (i.e., intelligible) the reflexive character of the action. The theorist is then interested in the rules that reflexively organize the accomplishment of practical actions.

Yet, the strong sense of irony is continually supplied in the work through the principled notion of how this "interest" differentiates theorist from member. In this way, every study affirms its own subscription to a principle of self-reflection as that interest in recollecting the practical action as an intelligible accomplishment. Garfinkel's work, by its very doing, continuously recommends itself as a principled mode of self-reflective discourse because, at the very least, he *is doing* what he *could* have found disinteresting. Further, it would be an enforceable and intelligible disinterest, and so that Garfinkel does what he does recommends the valid rather than expected.

If the differential interest of theorist and member is a resource for the ethnomethodological project, it is also its continuous topic regardless of the particular practice that is addressed. If the member is disinterested in self-reflection, there are always essentially good grounds for this disinterest, grounds that can be recapitulated as rules that enforceably provide for the practical treatment of practical action as the only way to formulate practices—that is, by taking for granted and orienting to the practice as unproblematic. That the theorist is not invidious (ironic in Garfinkel's sense) toward the member is given in his recognition of the way in which this injunction includes the practical action of inquiry itself: Inquiry understands itself as the same kind of practice as that which it formulates, and so it reflects upon itself adequately when it sees no essential difference between observer and observed. Of course, this humility is misguided, since the very possibility of Garfinkel's work rests upon the principle (the corrective and ironic claim) that interested self-reflection is (good, valuable) possible even *and* insofar as his interest unfolds as a feature of the very settings that tempt the many (including the theorist) into disinterest.

If self-reflection intends to re-lay the grounds of speech and language, what the theorist teaches the member is recapitulated in rules of usage. The member learns how an interested recollection of his practices is realized in a formulation of the normative order upon which those practices reflexively draw. If the member is not being "corrected," nevertheless, his "attention is turned" to a principled discourse in which he *could* engage as a discourse that is given and made possible by that selfsame normative order.

While Garfinkel's repudiation of a strong version of irony seems to him to be required by the reflexive imbeddedness of any inquiry in the very practical settings which it explores, this repudiation is a principled and ironic declaration upon the path open to inquiry. The proposal recommends that the self-reflective enterprise be limited by a concern with rules (with the accomplishment of intelligibility). Ethnomethodology only seeks to tell the member what he is (deeply, really) doing when he accomplishes whatever he does; though its interest in recapitulation is intelligible, it organizes its account so as to disregard—in principled ways—the contestability of its principle. It does so by equating the limits of rational inquiry with the statement of rules that organize the intelligibility of any practice without respect to anything other than the practitioner's interest in solving the problem of intelligibility.

When the member is formulated as acting under the auspices of the ethnomethodological interest, he is necessarily depicted as one who seeks to come to terms with the normative order (language) insofar as it generates the problem of its intelligibility. Members are seen as continuously reachieving enforceably intelligibile solutions to this order. The normative order is seen as a technical order, and the member (personified by the self-reflective inquirer) is seen as one who orients to problems and solutions posed by technical limitations of intelligibility.

Since self-reflection issues in a reformulation of rules of intelligibility, it teaches the member how a principled grasp of discourse (adequately applied) could result in an enforceably intelligible clarification of his environment (of his order). What the member learns is that in each and every case his oriented consultation of a rule to normalize the problematic distinction between "objective and indexical expressions" is both an essential feature of the intelligibility of his practice and a feature that is accomplished decisively in situations of choice. The member ironically related to is one who could realize his essential freedom (because what he is, is accomplished, is constructed, and this is his own responsibility). The limits of the teaching, then, are that an adequate grasp of the principled mode of discourse would result in a reflection upon self as a free actor (as an oriented and conventional actor). The self-reflection does not intend to create opportunities for reflecting upon limits of practical action but, rather, for understanding—*within these limits*—how the accomplishment of practical action confirms its irremediable conventionality.

Garfinkel's disregard of this principle in an oriented way is principled, which is to say that this disregard of the valid limit is a 'deep need' of the practical (enforceably intelligible) setting in which ethnomethodological inquiry originates as a feature of these selfsame settings. Facing up to the principle in a strong sense would be to invoke in unproblematic ways resources for normalizing these settings, and since the grounds of principle can never be made enforceably intelligible, we can only disregard the influence of principle by treating it as that which is necessarily inaccessible. This restatement of Simmel's conception of other repudiates alterity on the grounds of its not being needed. Other here is the normative order of language reconceived as the congeries of technical resources for accomplishing intelligibility; since the use of such resources is problematic in each and every case, the user's self-reflection must be limited by interests that are ultimately instrumental. An instrumental approach refuses to adjust to the ironic or principled question because it promises to go nowhere, i.e., it promises to go around in circles and never to be realized in a product. Anything other than instrumental interests (including anything other than their recognition as binding and valid) is to be disregarded on the principle that consideration of this question will make no difference to the work of clarifying the accomplishment of practical action. This is because questions as pervasive as this, which are inextricably raised by all work (by the act of speaking itself), will always be drawn upon in ways that are dispersive rather than enforceably intelligible.

As a teaching, Garfinkel's writings are intended to represent for the many a principled way of discoursing that limits itself to an interest in clarifying their practices (the practices of the many) as oriented accomplishments, i.e., as conventions. As a teaching, his work is intended to represent to and for the many what they are; that is, he represents them by *identifying* them. Because the limits of this identification reside in a formulation of their conventionality, we might say that he teaches the many that what they are is conventional. If the whatness of the many is their conventionality, they are not taught to aspire to anything other than this limit, because his repudiation of irony—his principled rejection of principle—requires that the question of what whatness is not be raised. Answers to this question cannot be envisaged as enforceably intelligible, and so they make no difference to what the many is. That the many is conventional is *what* they are.

The best the many can be—the highest challenge they can realize—is to develop the interest in self-reflection. They can seek to become like Garfinkel. But if Garfinkel only differs from them in the sense that he has this "deep need"—this interest in reflecting upon conventionality (in reflecting upon what they share in this particular sense)—then this difference is only technical, because what is shared is formulated in terms of the requirement that it be enforceably accessible to those very conventions, hence that it be limited by convention.

For Garfinkel, the member—convention—is "reflexive" and "incarnate":

> Practices consist of an endless, on-going, contingent accomplishment . . . done by parties to those settings whose skill with, knowledge of, and entitlement to the detailed work of that accomplishment . . . they obstinately depend upon, recognize, use and take for granted.[29]

That indexically accomplished membership is taken for granted means:

> In the actual occasions of interaction that accomplishment is for members omnipresent, unproblematic, and common-place.[30]

It is, therefore, always the case that "Members' inquiries are constituent features of the settings they analyze," inquiry always a member's inquiry, the difference between lay and professional always inessential or technical, because inquiry is just one among all other reflexive accomplishments. Any observer, however he is trained and whatever his intentions, can only be understood by reference to the encompassing nature and limits of practical action:

> *Wherever practical actions are the topics of study* the promised distinction and substitutability of objective for indexical expressions remains programmatic . . . In every actual case without exception, conditions will be cited that a competent investigator will be required to recognize, such that in *that* particular case the terms of the demonstration can be realized and nevertheless the demonstration be counted an adequate one.[31]

Thus, Garfinkel's examination of membership reveals it to be (1) indexically loose, (2) taken for granted. But what is essential here? If all inquiries are limited by practical action, and if practical action is always not only loose but taken for granted as well, has social inquiry been legislated out of existence? This is unlikely, since Garfinkel's own delineation of practical action is surely a claim to be some kind of inquiry.

Though loose and typically unproblematic, common sense nevertheless can be analyzed:

> For members doing sociology, to make that accomplishment a topic of practical sociological inquiry seems unavoidably to require that they treat the rational properties of practical activities as 'anthropologically strange.'[32]

To make the accomplishment of sociology a topic is to address its problematic nature, to think about what is habitually ordinary. We can be made to do this—any member can—through the attitude of anthropological estrangement or, as Garfinkel says, by seeing what we are doing now "as another first time." For Garfinkel, treatment as another first time is to express the 'awe' for commonplace accomplishment that is equivalent to the beginning of inquiry:

> In the unknown ways that the accomplishment [of social structure] is commonplace it is for our interests [as inquirers] an awesome phenomenon.[33]

That awe for the anthropologically strange can induce inquiry suggests the practical difference between the uninterested member and the interested one as a difference in receptiveness to awe: The uninterested member, the commonplace member, is limited by loose indexical practice and prefers to take that for granted; whereas the interested member, the awed member, is equally limited but is also aroused to represent that limit as a topic of inquiry. To establish the possibility of inquiry out of the whatness of membership, then, it is not that we must decide whether others are accessible in themselves, but first whether *we* are accessible to the natural awesomeness of achieved practical action.

According to this reading, disinterest is not essential to everyday life but a contingent resistance, more habitual than essential, which can be dissipated given the creation of certain estranging conditions that provoke awe and interest. It is thus possible to inquire, although inquirers continue to run into difficulty with commonplace action:

> The member of society uses background expectancies as a scheme of interpretation. With their use actual appearances are for him recognizable and intelligible as the appearances-of-familiar-events. Demonstrably he is responsive to this background, while at the same time he is at a loss to tell us specifically of what the expectancies consist. When we ask him about them he has little or nothing to say.[34]

The member is responsive (oriented to convention, to background expectancies) but is at a loss (speechless). Since the member-as-convention could be otherwise and need not be as he is, the awed inquirer's responsibility is to raise the circumstantial possibility that convention or membership or practical action may in fact be otherwise. And yet, it is not just a matter of will for the uninterested member, since when asked, he loses the faculty of speech. More is needed:

> Procedurally it is my preference to start with familiar scenes and ask what can be done to make trouble. The operations that one would have to perform in order to multiply the senseless features of perceived environments; to produce and sustain bewilderment, consternation, confusion . . . the socially structured affects of anxiety, shame, guilt and indignation; disorganized interaction should tell us something about how the structure of everyday activities are ordinarily and routinely produced and maintained.[35]

The special motive of the interested member is exercised to arouse the disinterested member by pursuing conditions that express the contingent and problematic nature of common convention. The inquirer, motivated by awe, must reproduce that awe by making the world seem anthropologically strange to common sense as well. It is only through the threat of loss of convention—of trouble—that the member can be made receptive and regain his lost speech. Analytically, then, common sense and inquiry are identical because they both could make topics of themselves, though they resist doing so until awed by the sheer contingency of convention (of themselves), which is ordinarily taken for granted and unspoken. The "interests" of each are generated, sustained, and limited by convention.

Thus ethnomethodology represents—speaks for—the multitude of uninterested but interesting common-sense courses of action. Ethnomethodology does not correct *multis* or treat *multis* ironically. The ethnomethodologist is only technically different, so how could he be principled about *this* difference? In a way, he does not know what is correct any more than the member, any more than convention knows; convention can know itself, but when itself is correct, it is enforceably intelligible, and such concerted meaning is indifferent to good. Boldly put, the enforceably intelligible nature of convention limits it to power and clarity. In fact, we have seen that making convention problematic is only to give voice to convention as a way of saying *how* convention is, not what it is. Convention is shown to be trusted in and through the times and places where convention is made problematic. Ethnomethodology's aim is to speak for the ordinary, which is ordinarily speechless, through the trouble that finally gains the attention of the ordinary. One might even say that it is his overwhelming trust in convention that makes the member uninterested in examining himself except as that trust seems to be put into question by trouble. Yet, ethnomethodology puts convention into question not to question convention but to affirm it, as a member would and does, and which ethnomethodology demonstrates in all the various problematic situations it has created among convention as the laborious but relentless work of reestablishing convention by "normalizing" trouble.

As the commonplace speaker, we might say that ethnomethodology is the mind of *multis*. Ethnomethodology speaks for practice rather than to practice, and in this sense it is the reflection of the member, the mirror that speaks for the image the mirror reflects. Ethnomethodology is the mind, speaker, representer, diplomat, statesman; it makes common sense visible, clarifies it, by speaking what fellow inhabitants of the commonplace know but are uninterested in formulating for themselves.

Social structure, which for ethnomethodology is the manifold accomplishment of countless practices, survives and prevails in the absence of ethnomethodology; the awe that induces inquiry is no more necessary than the taking for granted that inhibits it, and so ethnomethodology provides for its own lack of necessity as just another convention. Ethnomethodology's own self-reflection upon its place in loose common sense does not establish the necessity of speaking, because in this reflection speech follows in the trail of convention, and is always unnecessary and could always be otherwise.

Critical Theory

The problem of conceding the practical roots of self-reflection while making a place for it as something other than a recapitulation of convention has been addressed by a number of projects. This issue appears in the form of proposals for developing self-reflection upon convention that directs itself to something other than the principle of recapitulation, that is, as self-reflection that seeks to constitute itself as a critique of convention.

If we have noted how ethnomethodology masks its critique by claiming to eschew "corrections and irony" under the guise of being the paradigmatic practical account of practice—an account that is uncommitted to any principle other than this—we have also recognized the principled character of that claim. A critique of convention would proceed by recollecting the grounds of speech in language ironically, by constituting itself (by organizing its recollection) in full recognition of its own principled character. As discourse, such work would direct attention to itself. Such a critique would not enumerate its proposals as in a list because the incomplete character of any such enumeration conceals the very principles that it intends to explicate. Rather, by speaking in a decisive way about the conventions of the practice, the conventions animating the practice of the critique as its principled mode of discourse would become available as a feature of the discourse itself. Critical speech would introduce into its very discourse the question of discourse as itself a problem in order to revive the question of how we ought to speak.

> The theory specifies the conditions under which reflection upon the history of our species by members of this species themselves has become objectively possible; and at the same time it names those to whom this theory is addressed, who with its aid can gain enlightenment about their emancipatory role in the process of history. The theory occupies itself with reflection on the interrelationships of its origin and with anticipation of those of its application and thus sees itself as a necessary... moment within the social complex of life which it analyzes.[36]

Habermas's self-reflection is directed to specifying the conditions under which self-reflection becomes possible. Although it shares with ethnomethodology the interest in self-reflection, it is contrasted by its concern with reproducing self-reflection (in recreating a self-reflective actor). We say "*re*producing" and "*re*creating" because Habermas's writing testifies to the possibility of self-reflection as personified in his own discourse, for his writing represents the actualization of the self-reflective program that he intends to implement in the member. His interest must be understood as reproducing what *he* exemplifies—his principled mode of discourse—in the practical actor as a theory "which occupies itself with . . . anticipation of its . . . application." Garfinkel would claim no technical interest in reproducing such a theoretic actor, because this actualization can only be achieved by denying its own terms, by drawing in unexplicated ways upon those practical features of the practical settings that Habemas is seeking to overcome. Garfinkel would say that Habermas's project is irrational because it can only achieve what it intends by exemplifying the very "unreflective" reasoning it wants to cure.

But if it can be said that Habermas's interest in self-reflection is ambivalent about its own roots in the circumstantiality of practice, it can also be said that we have here a recognition that discourse needs to conceive of itself as guided by something other than the need to enforceably and intelligibly recapitulate practices. Critical discourse understands itself as essentially ironic or principled, even as this understanding is meant to reproduce itself in "those to whom the theory is addressed." On one level, the difference between Garfinkel and Habermas is that Garfinkel repudiates irony while always speaking ironically, whereas Habermas affirms the place of corrective and ironic discourse while always speaking in a way that is not ironic, while always speaking exegetically and hence technically about "conditions under which reflection ... has become objectively possible." In contrast to Garfinkel, Habermas accredits the ironic character of discourse as needing essentially to refer to itself and so to speak of its own principles:

> Critique understands that its claims to validity can be verified only in the successful process of enlightenment, and that means: in the practical discourse of those concerned. Critique renounces the comtemplative claims of theories constructed in monologic form, and in addition, discerns that all philosophy up to now, in spite of all its claims, also only presumes to have such a contemplative character.[37]

As opposed to "contemplation," critical theory's recognition of the conventionality of any and all discourse must include itself in that view; its actual recollective work must preserve the recognition of the achieved character of that work itself. Critical theory intends to preserve this recognition by making the convention upon which *it* depends visible *as* a convention (like his member, *this* is something in which Garfinkel is not interested).

It is not clear, though, how Habermas can accomplish this goal except through the renunciation of "monological form" for dialogue. But this means that if the renunciation is to be something other than an abstract critique of the failures of others, it must occur and show itself in the dialogue of Habermas. Everything then depends upon the question of what constitutes excellent discourse as a question that cannot be settled without raising it in the discourse itself. In other words, renunciation is only exegetical and abstract when it is not embodied in the narrative practice. This embodiment is difficult to discern in Habermas's own writings, however, since his exposition tends to recapitulate and explicate conditions *as if* the expository work is not animated by principle but "ruled" by the self-evident intelligibility of the subjects under discussion. If Habermas's own writing is intended to exemplify the narrative principle of self-reflection, it seems safe to say that his technical interest in reproducing a self-reflective actor is executed monologically by speaking to that actor as if he and Habermas confront what is being addressed (the language they share) as a self-evident matter that they could unequivocally consult as "specified conditions" for the "objectively possible." The repudiation of monologue is not embodied in this discourse itself. It acquires its critical character not by turning attention to itself and to its essential glossing practices—which Habermas himself requires as "reflection on its origin" and which actually and fundamentally reveal its animating principle—but proceeds instead to criticize speeches and texts for disregarding their own conventional impulses. There is no dialogue between origin and application because the origin is renunciated, and so *there seems to be no genuine respect for dialogue as the model of reflection.*

Habermas's notion of what such an oriented concern for one's own speech would look like (of what adequate discourse is) takes the form of an abstract recitation of concealed interests, assumptions, and beliefs in the works of others or in a descriptive enumeration of his own interests, assumptions, and beliefs. He is rooted in a mechanical conception of speech as interaction. This is all by way of saying that the question of what discourse is appears to be settled unequivocally by Habermas and used as a resource in a way that deflects attention from the question of how we discourse as a question worth raising. This is in spite of the recognition that Habermas continuously talks *about* discourse but always—we would say—from the perspective of one who takes his own discourse about discourse totally for granted.

> The sciences do not incorporate into their methodological understanding of themselves this basis of interest which serves as the *a priori* link between the origins and the application of their theories . . . I have sought to show how the relations of power embodied in systematically distorted communication can be attacked directly by the process of critique, so that in the self-reflection, . . . in the end insight can coincide with emancipation from unrecognized tendencies—that is, knowledge coincides with the fulfillment of the interest in liberation through knowledge.[38]

While this sounds similar to the critique developed by Husserl and Marx, it remains to be seen how *it* as a speech exemplifies such an "incorporation" *in its very speaking practices* or whether it can only generate lists of troubles and omissions in the texts it examines. This is to say that "critical theory" is truly critical only in the old-fashioned sense of the term: It identifies assumptions and interests in others as if *its* oriented work were disinterested, as if critical theory occurred only in response to these "problems." The interest we find in Garfinkel's work, an interest in the accomplishment of practical action, which is shown in that work as a respectful attempt to nurture and bring to appearance the deeply intelligible character of the practice, is glossed in the critique by critical theory which starts with such acomplishments as settled and "uninteresting" and then proceeds to discuss them externally. If Habermas concedes the principle animating his discourse whereas Garfinkel does not, this is only an abstract concession. As exemplified in his own writing, he, like Garfinkel's member, finds the reflexive character of practical action "uninteresting."

> Even if one admits that inherent within reason is also partisanship in favour of reason, still the claim to universality, which reflection as knowledge must make, is not to be reconciled with the particularity which must adhere to every interest, even that which aims at self-liberation.[39]

Habermas concedes the limited character of *his* discourse; that is, his partisan interest in reproducing the self-reflective actor is principled. In acknowledging how this principle originates in the "deep need" for a convention for speaking rationally about reason, he shows us how some conventions can be treated as more reasonable than others. What he recommends here is that the interest in self-reflection is essentially different from other interests. Yet, the image of self-reflection that is envisaged first appears only negatively, in the form of the member's "consciousness of this fact": that he *is* not self-reflective appears in a way that identifies the member's conception of what he is with the fact that he is not free:

> The logic of the self-reflection, which traces back the formative course of an ego's identity through all involutions of systematically distorted communications and brings this analytically to the ego's awareness, can be called 'dialectical' . . . but what is dialectical is then only the structure of compulsion that dialectical thought explodes by assimilating itself to it . . . Then, however, our problem is merely deferred. For the structure of this distorted communication is not ultimate; it has its basis in the logic of undistorted lanaguage communication.[40]

Thus, the self-reflective actor needs more than an historical consciousness of the "systematically distorted communication" that lives within him, because he requires a vision of ("undistorted") adequate or principled discourse.

> Discourse thereby renders possible the virtualization of claims to
> validity; this consists in our announcing with respect to the objects of
> communicative action . . . a reservation concerning their existence
> and conceiving of facts as well as of norms from the viewpoint of
> *possible* existence.[41]

If Garfinkel teaches the member that *what* he is is free, that he is
essentially conventional, then the member learns simultaneously that he is
not free to be anything other than conventional. Habermas wants to teach
the member that his freedom (his conventionality) resides in his having the
capacity to review all conventions so as to take responsibility for whatever
he decides to accept. Such a review can issue in the individuation and self-
identity of one who is sufficiently confident or mature to ground his choices
in the deliberation that is free from "systematically distorted communication"
(it is free from an unquestioning acceptance of claims). The member is
idealized as one who can deliberate upon his agreements, one who can
provide a logos for his agreements; consequently, his rationality consists
exclusively in his capacity to deliberate upon the claims of speech. Given
the essential conventionality of language, rationality can be reachieved as
prudence. As an idealization, critical self-reflection is the prudential
course of action, the action that deliberates upon the claims presupposed in
any speaking act.

Habermas's version of the difference between his project and that of
Garfinkel can be discerned through his distinction between "reconstruction"
and "self-reflection."

> As soon as we seek to clarify the structure of this reflection . . . its
> difference from scientific argumentation becomes clear . . . What is
> reasoned justification within the context of acts of reflection on
> oneself bases itself on theoretical knowledge which has been gained
> independently of the reflection on oneself, namely the rational
> reconstruction of rule systems which we have to master if we wish to
> process experience cognitively or participate in systems of discourse
> of action or carry on discourse . . . Self-reflection brings to consciousness
> those determinants of the self-formative process of cultivation and
> spiritual formation which ideologically determine a contemporary
> practice of action and the conception of the world. Analytic memories
> embrace the particulars, the specific course of self-formation of an
> individual subject . . . Rational reconstructions, in contrast, deal with
> anonymous rule systems, which any subjects whatsoever can
> comply with, insofar as they have acquired the corresponding
> confidence with respect to these rules. Reconstructions thus do not
> encompass subjectivity, within the horizon of which alone the

experience of reflection is possible. In the philosophical tradition these two legitimate forms of self-knowledge have generally remained undifferentiated and have both been included under the term of reflection. However, a reliable criterion of distinction is available. Self-reflection leads to insight due to the fact that what has previously been unconscious is made conscious in a manner rich in practical consequence: analytic insights intervene in life . . . A successful reconstruction also raises an 'unconsciously' functioning rule system to consciousness in a certain manner: it renders explicit the intuitive knowledge that is given with competence with respect to the rule in the form of 'know how.' But this theoretical knowledge has no practical consequences. By learning logic or linguistics I acquire theoretical knowledge, but in general I do not thereby change my previous practice of reasoning or speaking . . . Successful self-reflection results in insight which satisfies not only the conditions of the discursive realization of a claimed truth (or correctness) but in addition satisfies the condition of the realization of a claim to authenticity.[42]

Reconstruction is abstract: It is necessary but not sufficient for self-reflection, because self-reflection involves change, or, more adequately, *movement*, from ignorance to knowledge. But movement requires the formulation of causes or conditions. The problem confronted by the member *en route* to the actualization of self-reflection idealized in Habermas's conception of mature "self-identity" and "individuation" is to overcome the "logic of domination" embodied in all forms of "systematically distorted communication." Such an overcoming is not the end or realization of self-reflection, because the problem to be overcome is a *condition* (a means) that must be eliminated in order for self-reflection to be given an opportunity to realize itself. Self-reflection, then, is spoken about as if it were the end or good of a sequence of behaviors or movements.

Since all speech universalizes claims to validity by disregarding its own achieved origin (by conceiving of itself as evident or as true by nature), in treating prescriptions as "facts," it gives those who hear it no opportunity to imagine how it could be otherwise. In this way, speech acts *as if* there is nothing other to it, and so it sustains the hearer's propensity to orient to it as necessary and inevitable rather than conventional. This "logic of domination" is essential to all speech that does not invite attention to its own principled character. At this point, Habermas is most at home with the critique of the positive sciences from which he draws, in that he idealizes as a standard of adequate discourse a self-reflective engagement in conversation. Yet, this adequacy can only be a nostalgic notation of what is missing in the work of the positive sciences until it is translated into a discourse that exemplifies *in its own occurrence* the presence of what it takes to be missing. Because that exemplification is never present in Habermas, his critique can only be abstract. That he does not exemplify the presence in his own discourse of what is absent from the work he criticizes is shown in his intention to correct that work by producing (concretely, technically, behaviorally) the requirements he finds necessary yet absent. As we have seen, however, analytic requirements are the assumptive work of discourse and cannot be "produced" as events in the world, even as they can be referenced by those events.

What is needed by the member is to engage in a "relentless discursive examination of all claims to validity,"[43] yet he can only so engage if he has already mastered the competence idealized in the image of deliberative self-reflection. But this competence is precisely what the "relentless examination" is a preparation for, unless we admit that relentlessness actually exemplifies the end of self-reflection. At this point, it seems fair to say that the positive content that Habermas ascribes to self-reflection is exhausted by his conception of a "relentless discursive examination of all claims to validity" —this, then, is what self-reflection as prudential deliberation comes to.[44]

The competence envisaged in such an examination is idealized as the mastery of the system of rules that permits the actor to objectify his environment—the environment of speeches—by raising and challenging the claims to validity embodied in that environment. Such competence is depicted as an "ideal speech situation," because its mastery is the end toward which self-reflection aspires *and* a resource for making itself intelligible as aspiring toward that end.[45]

The "ideal speech situation" refers to a speaker's idealized use of language; it refers to an ideal speaker. The "ideal speech situation" is Habermas's version of other—of the normative order of language—which makes its "valid" and "binding" demand upon the actor (e.g., Habermas) as both his topic (how to achieve self-reflection) *and* his resource (that an understanding of how to achieve self-reflection presupposes its very mastery). As stated, though, the "ideal speech situation" appears as an abstract recommendation to be deliberative upon "claims to validity" without respect to what is good (what is valid). This is to say that the relentless deliberation that is to be applied to claims is not supplied with any origin in a standard that is itself valid. Rather, what is good and valid for self-reflection is the recognition that all claims to validity (that all claims to be good and valid) mask their own rhetorical interest. Habermas's ideal of self-reflection then teaches the speaker to distrust continuously all principled talk, on the grounds that only such continuous distrust will create his freedom.

If Habermas's "ideal situation of discourse" is a means for the achievement of self-identity and individuation, he stresses that it is still an idealization of competence. The technical interest in reproducing self-reflection needs to be satisfied by stating causal conditions for its occurrence: Yet, these conditions are formulated as the very same idealization they are designed to cause. Plainly, the "ideal speech situation" is another way of speaking about maturity, mastery, self-identification, and individuation. In this way, Habermas does not recognize the analytic status of his principle: that his recommendation of an ideal mode of discourse is an *analytic stipulation* that can only be misconstrued if it is understood as a technical program. While Habermas has a reasonable "deep need" to see his formulation actualized, this need leads him to speak about self-reflection as if it were an empirical problem, the problem of *becoming* self-reflective. In point of fact, the problem of self-reflection refers to the issue of exemplifying and embodying self-reflection actually and concretely in the discourse that speaks about it, not in the programmatic attempt to create concrete, actual, and virtualizable self-reflective human beings. The limits of self-reflection are always found in the exemplary work of the self-reflective discourse that points to itself—as its teaching—as that to which any man could aspire. But, criteria for assessing Habermas's self-reflective project can only be empirical, based on whether he can predict and control the *behavior* of self-reflection. It is in this sense that he does not exemplify and embody self-reflection; we are turned away from his speech to conditions that may or may not be accompanied by self-reflection.

In terms of our monograph, Habermas understands the analytic requirement of an oriented actor—recognized as such by everyone through Garfinkel—as a concrete and actualizable event. Habermas is evidently drawn to such an action only because he never accepted the terms and implications of the reformulations of the life-world as language out of his fear that this reformulation would dissolve inquiry into the practice of recapitulating conventions, i.e., as the practice of abstract "reconstruction." To revive the idea of a standard—of a ground for his principle—he thinks he needs to actualize his idealization in terms of criteria that depend upon the very same image of the relationship of language to the world against which the critique of the positive sciences was originally directed. Thus, whereas Garfinkel denies the need for principle and Habermas concedes it as an essential feature of speech, Habermas cannot conceive of grounding his principle except by recourse to technical actualization. Ultimately, for Habermas, rationality reduces to a positive conception of verification, or "proof."

Habermas teaches the member that domination can be resisted by learning to objectify the interests presupposed in discourse so as to be free to orient to them deliberatively. If the problem for the member is to develop mastery in the face of the forces that limit his capacity to achieve self-reflection, however, the achievement of such mastery is not a result or "effect" of the removal of these oppressive forces, it *is* the dissolution of the forces, nothing more. Because self-reflection has no positive content, it can only be expressed as a freedom *from* oppression and so as an opportunity to develop in ways that are unspecified. Critical theory then culminates in a liberal theory of self-reflection, which identifies freedom from domination with the deliberation upon "claims to validity" under the assumption that such deliberation will be emancipatory. In the absence of resources for engaging in the pursuit of any positive aim, the self-reflective actor has to draw upon his practical understanding of the practical features of settings untouched by his "relentless examination" (such as his mode of discourse itself, his technical interest in actualizing self-reflection, his idea of teaching as the paternal enforcement of intelligibility). If Garfinkel's fear of conceding the principled character of self-reflection is wrongheaded, we can now understand it as a concern that the consequences of such a concession are irrational, particularly insofar as some of those consequences are visible in critical theory. A theory that can only treat principle concretely and abstractly can only exempt its own discursive mode from examination.

NOTES

1. M. Heidegger, *Kant and the Problem of Metaphysics*, trans., J. S. Churchill, (Bloomington: Indiana University Press, 1968), p. 14.

2. See S. Karatheodoris, *The Logic and Ethic of Science* (Ph.D. diss., New York University, 1977).

3. P.L. Berger and T. Luckmann, *Social Construction of Reality* (New York: Anchor Books, 1967), p. 14f.

4. Berger and Luckmann acknowledge their indebtedness to Durkheim and Weber in that formulation of the "central question of sociological theory," *viz.*, "How is it possible that subjective meanings become objective facticities?" Ibid., p. 18. The discussion at this point is indebted to Karatheodoris, op. cit.

5. Ibid., p. 15.

6. See Karatheodoris, op. cit., for this development.

7. "I seem, then, in just this mere trifle to be wiser than [others], that what I do not know I do not think I know either." Plato, *Apology*, 21d, 8-10.

8. Cf., Meno's paradox that "a man cannot try to discover either what he knows or what he does not know. He would not seek what he knows, for since he knows it there is no need of the inquiry, nor what he does not know, for in that case he does not even know what he is looking for." E. Hamilton and H. Cairns, eds., *Collected Dialogues of Plato* (New York: Pantheon Books, 1966), p. 363. This can be seen to be reflected in the difficulty faced by Thomas Kuhn in his discussion of "paradigm change," when he says, "paradigm change cannot be justified by proof ... Though some scientists, particularly the older and more experienced ones, may resist indefinitely, most of them can be reached in one way or another." T.S. Kuhn, *Structure of Scientific Revolutions* (Chicago: University of Chicago, 1971), pp. 152f and 198ff.

9. Plato, *Meno*, 85d: *analabon autos ex autou ten epistemen.*

10. M. Weber, *The Theory of Social and Economic Organization* (Glencoe, Ill.: Free Press, 1947), p. 87.

11. T. Parsons, *The Structure of Social Action* (New York: McGraw-Hill, 1937), p. 636.

12. Ibid.

13. Ibid.

14. A. Schutz, *Phenomenology of the Social World* (Evanston, Ill.: Northwestern University Press, 1967), p. 26f.

15. Weber, op. cit., p. 95.

16. Ibid., p. 98.

17. K. Wolff, ed., *The Sociology of Georg Simmel* (Glencoe, Ill.: Free Press, 1950), p. 311.

18. H. Garfinkel, *Studies in Ethnomethodology* (Englewood Cliffs, N.J.: Prentice-Hall, 1967), p. 1.

19. Ibid., p. 4.

20. Ibid., p. 3.

21. Ibid., p. 7.

22. Weber, op. cit., p. 112.

23. Weber, op. cit., p. 124.

24. Although Weber tends to use validity as if it were "legitimacy" (i.e., enforceable intelligibility), we interpret "valid" in the (moral) sense of principle to be developed in subsequent sections.

25. Garfinkel, op. cit., p. 9.

26. We have in mind the strong sense of irony as developed in the Socratic project.

27. The Agnes story is a good example of this.

28. Weber, op. cit., p. 89f.

29. Garfinkel, op. cit., p. 1.

30. Ibid., p. 9.

31. Ibid., p. 6.

32. Ibid., p. 9.

33. Ibid., p. 10.

34. Ibid., p. 37.

35. Ibid., p. 38.

36. J. Habermas, *Theory and Practice* (Boston: Beacon Press, 1973), pp. 1-2.

37. Ibid., p. 2.

38. Ibid., p. 9.

39. Ibid., pp. 15-16.

40. Ibid., pp. 16-17.

41. Ibid., pp. 18-19.

42. Ibid., pp. 22-23.

43. J. Habermas, *Theorie der Gesellschaft oder Sozial Technologie*, Schramp, (Frankfurt: Surkhamp, 1971), p. 239.

44. Gadamer accurately locates this "enlightenment dogma" in his critique of Habermas by calling it an "anarchistic utopia" whose positive end is "the dissolution of all authority, all obedience," *Philosophical Hermeneutics* (Berkeley: University of California Press, 1977), p. 42.

45. Our discussion of Habermas is meant to emphasize issues that are relevant to our own issues in this text. Some readers have remarked that we do not adequately represent Habermas's own understanding, and we are presently taking this into consideration.

The Social Order Problem Again:
The Adequacy of an Account

The central issue to have emerged from our discussion of self-reflection is the problem of how self-reflection upon the action of inquiry can provide a rational appraisal of itself, since any such appraisal is "merely" an extension or example of self-reflection.

> If our aim is to provide an adequate reading, formulation or description for a stretch of talk, the extent to which this is a fruitful analytic exercise will depend on whether we can extract unambiguously one formulation rather than a set of alternative formulations . . . .[1]

If this writer is saying that our "deep need" is for formulations that are sufficiently powerful and clear to enable them to be enforceably agreed upon, we would of course object. We can agree upon the need for a rational assessment of our formulative work without accepting a principle here that equates 'adequacy' with the lack of ambiguity. We have a deep need to assess our formulative work, a need that crystallizes under the auspices of our recognition that such work is always one of many possibilities. In fact, we utilize this recognition to organize our formulations in such a way as to invite attention to their *being* one of many. We do this not out of a sense that our formulation is interchangeable with the others that are possible, i.e., that they are interchangeably one of many, but to show how *(because* of its being one of *many)* we have decided upon it for reasons that are good.

Our deep need, then, is to embody in our formulative work our good reasons for doing as we do. These reasons are *shown* as the intelligibility of our analyses—as they are embodied, they are shown as our good reasons. In each of the analyses proposed in this project, the question of adequacy is invited to become the joint responsibility of the analyst and the reader as (1) the task of understanding how the analytic principle is exemplified in the work and (2) the task of clarifying the status of the principle as a recommendation concerning how we ought to engage in a self-reflection upon our discourse. Unambiguous answers cannot be given to these questions, because both question and answer arise within the life-world as a feature of the essentially "open" texture of language.[2] Adequate discourse would then be that which provides for itself in the face of this texture, not by claiming to be unambiguous, but by offering up its grounds as its principled claim to adequacy: such a discourse would ironically draw attention to itself as rational rather than as "unambiguous."

Of course this statement of our conception of rationality—as a "criterion" of adequate discourse—is still ambiguous. But this only means that whether or not it is rational (in the particular case) depends upon particular circumstances that can be indefinitely modified and expanded; it only means that "rational" is not a word whose normal use we can fix without reservation, that it is not the kind of usage that can be intelligibly fixed in every particular case and to the satisfaction of every particular member of this species.[3]

The problem, then, is one of supplying rational grounds for formulative work insofar as, by virtue of its origin in the life-world of practical action, all formulative work assumes in unanalyzed ways the adequacy of its own principled mode of discourse. We have said that this is not a "problem" or a paradox but is, rather, a feature of any oriented relationship to language. Consequently, the task of self-reflection is to turn attention to its principle as a matter that can be contested.

> On the one hand, the meaning of words and utterances is . . . bound up with and occasioned by the particular contexts in which words are uttered. Moreover the meaning of words is imprecise in any strict sense [i.e.] there are various difficulties which are encountered in the arguments of those who claim that the meaning of words and utterances can be represented by a set of criterial features or a set of rules. Talk, then, is a form of *glossing* . . . the analysis of meaning is never exhausted by a simple analysis of the words uttered . . . .
> On the other side of the paradox we have the fact that talk is experienced by participants as an ordered phenomenon.[4]

Although Wootton understands social order as a "paradox," by now we should recognize his dilemma. Why should the fact that talk is always glossed be paradoxical vis-à-vis its being "experienced by participants as an ordered phenomenon"? This "paradox" refers to what is known historically as the social order problem, and the commentator misconstrues the *analytic* character of the problem.

It is not as if we have "on the one hand" language and "on the other hand" what participants "experience" language to be, because—as we have said—the idea of language collects *both* the fact that it glosses and the usages ("responses") of members that exemplify that very fact. Indeed it is *because* the speaker "glosses" that he can experience his talk as "an ordered phenomenon."

When the self-reflective actor is imagined not as one who seeks to "solve" the (dualistically conceived) "problem of order" but as one who seeks to recollect how an oriented grasp of circumstances accomplishes that very orderliness, then he is seen not as an exception to "on the one hand . . . talk . . . is a form of glossing" but as an *example* of it, as one whose accomplishment of order documents the essentially elliptical character of language.

In self-reflective work, the glossing practices of analysts in formulating their material need to be explicated as a feature integral (essential) to their accomplishment of an intelligible formulation. That the analyst's work glosses only means that in any particular instance it shows its oriented commitment to not wanting to speak about certain resourceful understandings that it uses to accomplish its work.

This disregard is not mischievous; rather, it shows what the analyst as a practical actor thinks is not worth speaking about as that which he had *decided* not to speak about for good and positive reasons. This decision— insofar as it makes reference to his principled conception of adequate discourse—testifies to the positive character of his limits and should not be conceived as an omission or a deficiency unless we first appreciate its oriented and principled character. In showing this, the analyst reveals a standard he employs in deciding upon the limits of his discourse.[5]

Because "all talk . . . is a form of glossing," self-reflection does not differ on that score. What matters is what it is that self-reflection shows a decision to be silent about (note though that this silence *is shown* actively in the talk, and so, in that sense, the silence is spoken). We have suggested that if some decide to be silent about technique (power, clarity, intelligibility, method), others are silent about principle (value, *telos,* reason). Furthermore, if what one is silent about is taught to the member as what he should be silent about in order to do the action of speaking well, then he is instructed in an action of positive disregard, and the lesson will hold implications for moral action.

To say that the "meaning of words and utterances is . . . bound up with and occasioned by the particular context in which words are uttered" is to state—as de Saussure did—that signification is arbitrary. The arbitrary character of signification means, first, that its origins in particular circumstances are fortuitous (are indifferent to orientation, aim, intention) and, so, are always experienced as an otherness ("as a heritage of the preceding period"[6] that cannot be fixed rationally[7]; and second, that it is essentially open to modification—"no force guarantees the maintenance of a regularity when established on some point."[8] So the idea that "meaning can never be exhausted by a simple analysis of the words "suggests that terms acquire their value (according to de Saussure) through the particular and arbitrary conventions embodied in the relations between terms (relations that are external to the terms, to speech).[9]

Yet, the fact that signification is done is possible only because the speaker imposes and limits the multiplicity of possibilities for speaking as he does. There is nothing "paradoxical" about this limitation, for it is a feature of the multiplicity itself, and its possibility is actually shown in the analyses of language as that recollective work that provides a sense of how such limitation can be done.[10] The very possibility of self-reflection confirms the way the speaker limits multiplicity, and so the theorist's conception of the arbitrary and particular origins of speech is a reconstruction of the "problem" for which intelligible speech is always imaginable as a solution. Thus, the theorist's version of the member's "problem" as an idealization is simultaneously his identification of the theoretic problem.

The social order problem is the self-reflective actor's version of the member's "problem," when the member is construed as if he is in position to orient to the problem that, in actuality, only the self-reflective actor is consciously oriented to (to the problem of self-reflection). But we must be careful here of the use we make of "being conscious."

> The system is . . . complex . . . (it) can be grasped only through reflection: the very ones who use it daily are ignorant of it.[11]

The social order problem says that intelligible speech requires a solution to the problem of language—of limiting multiplicity—on the part of every single actual and concrete speaker and that such solutions depend upon speakers' oriented knowledge. While the recollection of such knowledge is available to all speakers, it is the eccentric enterprise of self-reflection that has the "deep need" to take up this topic—to recollect itself. In proceeding, the self-reflective actor has three alternatives:

1. He can describe speaking practices diachronically.[12]

2. He can recapitulate or "reconstruct" the knowledge (the values, identifications) that organize speakers' practices of limiting multiplicity.

3. He can seek to respond to such irrationality (multiplicity, arbitrariness) rationally, by turning attention to the need to treat such limitation as expressions of matters of principle upon which all speakers could and should deliberate.

We see that the social order problem really makes reference to the problem of criteria: how to provide an unambiguous formulation given the fact that talk essentially glosses. But now we understand that we cannot provide such a formulation, because "ambiguity" is essential and not incidental to talk.

How can we achieve satisfaction, given the fact that our work is never unambiguous? How can we achieve definitive formulative results, given the fact that our formulative work is essentially open to modification? To attempt to reduce ambiguity would be unnatural, because it would reproduce the solution of the positive sciences, which seek to reform ambiguity and hence to violate the life-world.

If language is essentially synchronic, then its oriented usage (*parole*) is always accomplished as a conventional solution to its horizon of "open-ended" decidable matters and possibilities. To propose "criterial features" or a "set of rules" for adequate discourse would be another "form of glossing," and the expectation of "hypotheses" is premature, since it depends upon so general a conception of the member as to disregard both his particular circumstances and the particularity of the circumstances that surround our contact—as inquirers—with him. Nevertheless, because we repudiate general criteria in these forms does not mean that (1) we do not have expectations, problems, or questions (rather than "hypotheses"); we have directed normative interests; or that (2) we do not have principles or standards of adequate discourse (rather than "criterial features"); we have various senses of how adequacy can be *shown* in discourse rather than spoken through a general enumeration of "criteria."[13]

Three Types of Ambiguity

The work we have reviewed accepts ambiguity by transforming it into a topic. Because Garfinkel recognizes ambiguity as a resource, he accepts as his limit the task of reporting upon how its reduction is treated by members as unambiguous, as if it were perfectly clear. Garfinkel finds this "awesome," and his project is designed to recapitulate such achievements. He judges his recapitulative work adequate when its own ambiguity is minimal; that is, when it can be accepted by any practical actor as an account of what we are doing when we do a thing at all. In contrast, because Habermas understands ambiguity only as a topic (and so he exempts his own discourse from that recognition), he tries to reduce it by developing and implementing in the species the capacities and skills for critical assessment.

Habermas's paternalist program seeks to enable the member to reduce ambiguity by critically evaluating and comparing "claims to validity." He contends that a claim to validity (for example, that his own work is adequate) is strengthened when that which such a claim recommends is enforced in the behavior of the species, i.e., in actual concrete persons. His notion of "proof" recalls Weber's distinction between adequacy on the level of meaning and causal adequacy in his argument that the meaning of self-reflection can only be enforceably agreed upon when it is produced or actualized. He tries to synthesize the life-world as language and descriptive adequacy by reformulating the problem of self-reflection as the relationship between ideal (language) and action (behavior). For Habermas, the social order problem appears in the problem of enforcing "theory" in the conduct and behavior of the species. Naturally, this repeals the critique of the positive sciences by importing back into that reformulation an empirical conception of the relationship between language and the world.[14]

It will be instructive to briefly consider some work of Barthes for the way in which it speaks this problem. Barthes' recognition of the extent to which formulative work participates in the very conventions that it intends to formulate is more forthright then Garfinkel's disinterest or Habermas's criticalness.

His notion of "mythologies" has apparent affinities to the program of ethnomethodology and critical theory. In speaking of his work as animated by "impatience at the sight of the 'naturalness' (with which) reality is dressed up . . . even though it is determined by history,"[15] he constructs the member—which for him is the exemplary practical mode of self-reflection—as showing a "confusion of nature and history."[16] Barthes' critique draws upon the same understandings of the tradition we have discussed in this proposal, in the sense that he wants to overcome the type of self-reflection that treats what is accomplished or achieved as if it is necessary (inevitable, natural). Regardless of whether this "illusion" is a function of practical disinterest in the reflexive character of practical action (Garfinkel) or of the dependencies and nonfreedom of the member (Habermas), it can only be addressed by analyzing the routine and regular repetitions or products that it realizes in the artifacts of popular culture and everyday life. By focusing upon what he chooses to call the mythological structure of everyday speech, Barthes seeks to recollect the principled mode of discourse that animates popular speech as a feature of the same "logic of domination" of which Habermas speaks: Popular speech is a feature of the interest in universalizing prescriptions *as* a suppression of history.

Yet, Barthes wonders uneasily about his principle: "Is there a mythology of the mythologist? No doubt, and the reader will easily see where I stand."[17]

If the analyst (mythologist) is a practical actor, his formulative work is accomplished as a feature of his unexplicated and decisive use of what he "deeply needs" (wants, knows) in regard to the settings he intends to formulate. As in Garfinkel, this is not denied, yet something more is needed to preserve the distinctive character of self-reflection. Perhaps this "something more" is supplied in the remark that "the reader will easily see where I stand"; perhaps self-reflection is intended as that discourse that enables (and, indeed, orients to inviting) the reader (the interlocutor) to "see where I stand."

If Garfinkel is disinterested in this, if he does not have this need, it is because he intends his speeches to provide intelligible versions of where he stands insofar as they are produced as descriptions of practical actions that have a degree of autonomy vis à vis any principle. Garfinkel's adherence to descriptive standards of adequacy makes the question of "where I stand" gratuitous, for it is not a question that needs to be asked: one must only consult the work, the researches, to see how the commitment is realized and embodied directly in its products. In a sense, Garfinkel's commitment must show itself in its products, or we could not orient to the commitment as we have in this proposal. Still, whether or not we are "interested" in that question is of no interest to Garfinkel, since he requires that we treat his work under the auspices of a standard of descriptive adequacy.

Oppositely, Habermas is quite concerned to situate himself through inventories of "principles." He assumes the interesting character of providing for himself by acting as if self-reflection is equivalent to an external description of self that will satisfy that interest.

If Barthes appears to recognize that where he stands is the actual and deep topic of his work, he senses that his discourse is reflective upon its own status, that it is reflective upon discourse itself. As Jameson puts it:

> It is axiomatic that a philosophy which does not include within itself a theory of its own particular situation, which does not make a place for

some essential self-consciousness along with the consciousness of the object with which it is concerned, which does not provide for some basic explanation of its own knowledge at the same time that it goes on knowing what it is supposed to know, is bound to end up drawing its own eye without realizing it.[18]

But the inclusion of the action of self-reflection in the reflection is not an incidental feature, as it is to Garfinkel and (deeply) to Habermas; *it is what the discourse is about.* This is to say that the discourse of self-reflection unfolds as an attempt to reflect upon itself, to reflect upon its own discourse as an instance of the question of what discourse is and as an example of an answer to that question. In any study, the member (the material) is formulated in relation to the orientation that is imputed to it vis-à-vis a standard of adequate (normative) self-reflection, which the analyst exemplifies in his very action of narration. No matter what the substantive character of the topic, the analytic parameter of oriented action requires the actor's intelligible accomplishment of whatever he does to be made intelligible through his resourceful use of the environment that the analyst ascribes to him as his relevant limit. It is not that inquiry is about, say, unemployment and incidentally relevant to self-reflection: rather to talk about unemployment always assumes of it an oriented character, and thus it is always assumed to represent some solution to a standard that its "adequate" exemplification would grasp.

Barthes' solution to the problem of exemplifying self-reflection and discourse in a way that would exempt him from the charge of conventionalism (from being a 'mythologist' not essentially different from any other) is strange. "What I claim is to live to the full the contradiction of my time, which may well make sarcasm the condition of truth."[19]

Whereas Garfinkel's repudiation of irony is intended to rebut the charge that he is "sarcastic," he can only do this by accepting his place as a representative or mouthpiece (a scientific spokesman) for the many. In contrast, Habermas can only comprehend irony as exegetical criticism. Neither Garfinkel nor Habermas has a version of irony as (in part) an aesthetic feature of narration that draws attention to the principle of self-reflection itself by inviting the reader to see "where I stand." This is to say that both Garfinkel and Habermas are disinterested in discourse except insofar as they need to use it either to describe practical actions, in the one case, or to affirm criticalness, in the other.

But can sarcasm be the "condition of truth" of our time? To live "to the full contradiction of my time" is to have the deep need to engage in self-reflection in full recognition of the inescapably practical and conventional character of that engagement. Yet, "sarcasm" is as parasitical and detached as the disinterested contemplation and description of the positive sciences, for it never risks itself. Irony is differnt from sarcasm; irony draws attention to itself—to its proposal or principle—as that which is worth striving for because it is good. The idea that sarcasm is the "condition of truth" is a melancholy statement of principle for the practical action of self-reflection.

> Human knowledge can participate in the becoming of the world only through a series of successive metalanguages, each one of which is alienated in the very moment that determines it. We express this in dialectical and formal terms: when he speaks of the rhetorical signified in his own metalanguage, the analyst inaugurates (or reassumes) an infinite type of knowledge-system: for if it had happened for someone else (someone else, or himself later on) to undertake an analysis of his writing and to attempt to reveal its latent content, it would be necessary for this someone to have recourse to a new metalanguage, which would in his turn expose him: and the day will inevitably come when structural analysis will pass to the rank of an object-language and be absorbed into a more complex system which will explain it in turn. This infinite construction is not sophisticated: it accounts for the transitory and somehow suspended objectivity in research, and confirms what we might call the Heraclitean characteristics of human knowledge, at any point when by its object it is condemned to identify truth with language.[20]

Our reformulation of self-reflection as the deep need of speech to recollect—in the narrative action of discourse—its ground in language raises the question of what adequate recollective work is (what adequate discourse is). This question can only be addressed by accepting the full implications of the reformulation of the life-world as language which means that it can only be addressed by accepting the place of self-reflection as a social action that depends upon the particular circumstances of conventions. We have suggested that adequate recollective work (adequate theory) will show its adequacy not through any particular substantive proposal or thesis or by resigning to its own conventionality or dissolving in sarcasm, but by drawing attention to the way in which it speaks as a recommendation of principle (of value).

How we speak about our material merely exemplifies and extends this problem, because in speaking *about* it (in formulating the grounds of its practices), we speak *to* it about how we need to proceed in order to speak well. Since our formulative work depends upon our drawing in unanalyzed ways upon understandings we all share, each of our formulations exposes itself as a proposal for, and exemplification of, a different opportunity for relating to the language we share, an opportunity whose realization is presumably good and valuable.

NOTES

1. A. Wootton, *Dilemmas of Discourse* (London: Allen and Unwin Ltd., 1975), p. 19.
2. See F. Waismann, "Verifiability" and "Language Strata" in A. Flew, ed., *Logic and Language* (New York: Anchor Books, 1965).
3. To those who equate validity with power and clarity, such a standard appears "unclear and arbitrary, since any particular presentation is always open to further modification." See comments upon the work of Blum and McHugh by Wootton, *op. cit.,* p. 102.
4. Wootton, op. cit., p. 59.
5. This is a feature of what Heidegger calls the self-concealing character of language; Gadamer speaks of it as "self-forgetfulness." The self-concealing feature of language tells us that omissions are not necessarily the result of external conditions or of certain "intentions," because it is essential that speech be unable to appropriate its origins in language to itself in another speech, i.e., that the otherness of language cannot be unambiguously represented to itself in a way of which modification is not thinkable. This is why it is misleading to link self-reflection to the removal of "puzzles," as if the deep need for self-reflection is not an available possibility in any action.
6. F. de Saussure, *Course in General Linguistics* (London: Fontana/Collins, 1974).
7. Ibid., p. 73.
8. Ibid., p. 92; de Saussure connects these characteristics around the conception of language as oriented and motivated (synchronic) and speech as indifferent to value (diachronic).
9. Ibid., pp. 130–131, for the development of the discussion that signification depends upon relationships (a whole) that cannot be reduced to signification itself.
10. The social order problem becomes a "paradox" that is converted into the issue of how to develop "unambiguous" formulations when the essentially synchronic character of language noted by de Saussure, Wittgenstein, Heidegger, Derrida, and others is not grasped. Even philosophers who claim to accept the "linguistic turn"—(F.R. Rorty, ed., *The Linguistic Turn* (Chicago: The University of Chicago Press, 1967)—surreptitiously long for a "set of criterial features or a set of rules" to reduce ambiguity, i.e., to resolve the "evaluation" problem. One need only compare, for example, the essays on language in H.G. Gadamer, *Truth and Method*: (London: Sheed & Ward, 1975) and *Philosophical Hermeneutics* (Berkeley: University of California Press, 1974) with Strawson's conception of discourse in *Meaning and Truth* (Berkeley: University of California Press, 1974), to appreciate the stark difference.
11. De Saussure, op. cit., p. 73.
12. Cf., de Saussure, op. cit., on how a diachronic conception of language reduces the oriented action of language to linguistic behavior *(parole)* or usage.
13. Perhaps we might think of an adequate account not as a particular type of speech but more like a conversation or relationship among friends in which nothing is settled "unambiguously" and unequivocally, but rather, where the terms, conditions, and principles of the discourse are progressively clarified through the discourse itself as a matter in which all can engage and upon which they can reflect—that is, as the topic of their discourse *and* as a resource for its progression. Then how could we tell when the discourse is adequate? We could not, if "telling" means "enumerating criterial features"; but are there not other possibilities?

14. See Gadamer's reaction: "it is absolutely absurd to regard the concrete factors of work and politics as outside the scope of [language]": op. cit., p. 31.

15. R. Barthes, *Mythologies* (London: Palladin Press, 1972), p. 11.

16. Ibid., p. 11.

17. Ibid., p. 12.

18. F. Jameson, *The Prison House of Language: A Critical Account of Structuralism and Russian Formalism* (Princeton, N.J.: Princeton University Press, 1977).

19. Ibid., p. 12.

20. R. Barthes, *Systeme de la Mode* (Paris: Seuil, 1967), p. 293.

Theorizing as Morally Oriented:
The Notion of Pedagogy

All projects on self-reflection can be read as programs of morally oriented education. This is because the principled mode of self-reflective discourse that personifies "adequate theory" in each program, no matter what its particular substance, is embodied in the discourse itself as both a resource for its work *and* a latent possibility for the member. The principled mode of self-reflective discourse, which this work is intended to exemplify in its very own narrative, always and essentially pictures language as a normative order (as exemplified in the grasp of correct speaking displayed by the analyst) to which the member can orient. What is pictured is some version of a good relationship to language—some version of language use or of discourse—as a valid and binding order.

In formulating rules to guide the accomplishment of practices, the inquirer orients to and uses rules in his writing and speaking in a way that is intended to exemplify what adequate usage (what an adequate grasp) is. In formulating any topic, the inquirer appears as an oriented user of speech who acts under the auspices of a normative order of enforceably intelligible usage that is good. This normative order is evoked through his inquiry (it is shown in his work) as a way of exemplifying how to speak well (intelligibly) about that which both he and the member are in position to speak well. What is also shown in his work is the principled nature of the way in which the inquirer speaks well, his decisive recommendation as to the limit that is language.

For Garfinkel and Habermas, the limits of value are discerned in competence, in the capacity of deliberate comprehensively upon the achieved character of speech. These inquirers idealize self-reflection as the competence entailed by the use of rules for identifying in enforceably intelligible ways the conventional sources of practices. Education is achieved by the application and execution of such competence as personified in the performance of the theorist as a self-reflective actor. The ideal to which these theorists subscribe, then, is that of the member as intelligent *and* of his self-reflective limits as the exercise of intelligence.

We have discussed the nature of deep need as one that resonates with language as the source and limit of the whole. Being source and limit, language is not conceived to be a cause and barrier for behavior, but rather to lay out the possibility for self-reflection.

It has developed in our examination so far that the deep need of theorizing is for an actor who is oriented to the life-world as an enforceably intelligible world that offers the possibility of principled speaking.

In other words, the life-world is one in which the actor needs, and knows he needs, to be oriented. We can always ask of a theoretic actor: "What is needed by that actor to be what he is?"

There remain several senses of need, conceived as that which is made essential for and by an oriented actor:[1]

1. In order to do *x* reflectively, it is essential to be seen to do *x*; *x* must be intelligible to any reciprocally oriented actor.

2. In order to do *x* reflectively, it is essential that *x* be reasonable; *x* must be enforceable to any reciprocally oriented actor.

3. In order to do *x* reflectively, it is essential that *x* be (principled) undertaken for its essential desirability; *x* must be moral to a reciprocally oriented actor.

Intelligibility orients the actor to resourceful use and control of action as an interactive or symbolic transmission among alters. Here the actor must theorize the "meaning" of his action for the collective in which he participates as a meaning that he may express, but that depends upon ratification by the collective if it is to be realized as valid, true, or social. The actor must know, express, and work to control the reception of his and others' actions as formulably intelligible ones.

Some intelligible actions may nevertheless be unacceptable, however; in some cases (e.g., Weber, ethnomethodology), whatever is social must be enforceable if the social is to sustain itself. Here the actor needs to orient to the need of the life-world for the order that attends upon thoughtful compliance. It is not simply that the actor conforms (this would not require any reflection), but that the actor *wants* to conform, and so the reasonability of his behavior is for this actor a deep need rather than a mechanical or coerced reaction to demand.

Thus, the deep need of intelligibility and enforceability is for an actor who is competent, resourceful, and even masterly in his use and expression of convention. He is willing, and willing to be communicative, regardless of difficulties in particular and local circumstances, and in spite of the failure, deviance, and ambiguity that may occur in those circumstances. He is oriented to the life-world as one that itself needs to be skillfully represented in his own actions as an icon of the possibilities and limits of convention. There is thus something essentially moral in the conception of an actor who orients to the need to intelligibly represent the life-world in his own actions in the sense that he is seen as wanting to undertake the action of representing. Yet, the moral component of his action is only seen derivatively—in doing well what*ever* he does—for his moral limit is fundamentally reflected in undertaking to represent the life-world. He orients to his need to maintain and enforce intelligibility.

For some, the issue of morality is the issue of doing practice well:

> A statement of what we *must* do (or say) has a point only in the context (against the background) of knowledge that we are in fact doing (or saying) a thing, but doing (saying) it—or running a definite risk of doing or saying it—badly, inappropriately, thoughtlessly, tactlessly, self-deceivingly etc.; or against the background of knowledge that we are in a certain position or occupy a certain office or station, and are behaving or conducting ourself inappropriately, thoughtlessly, self-deceivingly . . . The same is true of statements about what we may do, as well as those . . . about what we should do, or what we are or have to do, or are supposed to do, and about one sense of what we can do; these are all intelligible only against the background of what we are doing or are in a position . . . to do. These . . . verbs . . . cannot stand as the main verb of a sentence . . . their use is not one of prescribing some new action to us, but of setting an act which is antecedently relevant to what we are doing or to what we are . . . there is no question of going from 'is' to 'must' but only of appreciating which of them should be said when . . .

> To tell me what I must do is not the same as to tell me what I ought to do . . . 'Ought' unlike 'must,' implies that there are alternatives; 'ought' implies that you can, if you choose, do otherwise. This does not mean merely that there is something else to do which is in your power, but that there is one within your right. But if I say truly and appropriately, 'you must . . .' then in a perfectly good sense nothing you then do can prove me wrong . . . This may be made clear by considering one way principles differ from rules. Rules tell you what to do when you do the thing at all; principles tell you how to do the thing well, with skill or understanding . . . Both the rules which constitute playing the game, and the 'rules' as maxims which contribute to playing the game well, have their analogues in ordinary moral conduct.[2]

If morality is to seek to practice well, then morality is made to follow upon practice, because it is practice that sets the conditions for moral action. Convention remains the limit, and moral action must find its place within convention. In this circumstance, convention is not reflected upon except technically (e.g., "How must it be done to be done well?" rather than "Ought it to be done?"), and the idea of doing the action at all is reduced to its intelligibility, efficacy, enforceability.

The problem here is that to do something well (to be moral in *that* way) presupposes that one has already undertaken to do it, which confuses the best ways to care with the need for care. The best ways to care for convention, presumably, are derivative of the need to care at all, and the need to care is not identical with intelligible and enforceable means for caring. It would be for us a moral failure to equate doing a practice well with all moral action, although doing a practice well expresses moral comitment to the action *if* that action is decisive—if the action originates in care, and if it is not merely carefully compliant action. We might say, recalling our discussion of convention as that which could be otherwise: that it could be otherwise is the very issue that a morally oriented actor will consider in taking up conventionally practical action, and it is this knowledge that gives him the reserve and opportunity to be decisive, responsible, and the agent of his action. In other words, the morally endowed actor can recognize that he lives in convention but need not be of convention, because it is he who may (ought to) reauthorize convention through the agency of his decision to undertake or not. Prior to the question of doing it well or poorly is: whether to do it at all.

Part of the culture of children, for example, is the matter of learning to write. It is said that there is an appropriate time for this; at certain ages, children are not ready or in position to learn, and this is often taken to mean that they lack the skills or motives to do it well. But if we think of children's culture as oriented action, it is just possible that they would not write well because they have other things to do—they are engaged in the acts and needs of too rich a public life to begin the more egocentric, self-contained activity of formal writing. To set out to do something is partly the issue of setting out to do it well (to want to do it, according to our examination of enforceability), but of course we must first *set out* to do it if we are not to deny that action is oriented through and through.

To do something well is therefore to presuppose the nature of *what* one is doing well as something other than a technical choice. The whatness of an action includes that one undertakes to do it, and one can undertake to do it because (1) it is expected and (2) it is right.[3] If one undertakes what is right, it is difficult to imagine that one would want to do it poorly. That is, to undertake something because it is right seems to require that one try to do it well. And yet to undertake to do it can be for other than right reasons—because it is expected regardless of right—and here trying to do well is more problematic. Any actor, then, can endow his action with right and/or expected grounds, which means that for any actor this itself can become a problematic issue of orientation. We need to develop an oriented actor who can theorize about the auspices of his commitments to action, auspices that are not always identical unless one assimilates what is right to what is expected.

It is difficult to imagine that joy could animate practice if we assimilate principle to expectation. We affirm that the life-world leaves a place for an actor who can enjoy what he does, that his best times are not those when he could only be stimulated by obligation. This is the problem with enforceable intelligibility, if not with all modern sociology: It offers no room for the actor who wants to do it because he wants to do it. He only wants to do it because it is expected, and so he does not authorize so much as comply when he acts. The trouble with the idea of "motivated compliance," for example, is that it provides no grasp of an actor who could enjoy his circumstances. The social order problem requires only an actor who is motivated to comply, howsoever this linking might be accomplished in the life-world and whatsoever the actor's understanding of this linking might be. *Our* principle, then, is to affirm that self-reflection is necessary so long as that necessity is also understood as desirable. Our actor needs to enjoy self-reflection as a need that is desirable. This is another way of saying that the need for self-reflection is not mechanical, and so the actor who would orient to this need could not do so mechanically.

The actor who is reserved toward convention—who, though he respects the necessity of convention, does not treat it as the limit—is oriented to the nature of his undertakings as well as to the quality of their expression. He first puts convention itself at risk (even while there may be risks to his own repute as a conventional member when he does so), because what is decisive for him is the integrity of his affirmation of the practical actions he undertakes *as* he undertakes them. What he does he wants to do well, certainly, but he also knows that in doing it well, he is affirming the very thing he is doing as worthy of doing. The morality of doing something well or poorly is thus derivative morality, in that it is only a bona fide of some already-affirmed moral commitment to undertake.

In general, then, one can fail to theorize undertaking, or one can fail, having so theorized, to accomplish the undertaking as a result of the existence of conditions of failure in the world (e.g., lack of skill, lack of resources, lack of control). These are not equivalents even though both are poor: the first is to fail morally, the second to fail conventionally. They are failures of different kinds, failures of principle and failures of practice.

It is not that principles are not practices—they are—but we recognize that principled practice can fail without being a failure of principle; that practice can succeed without being a morally committed practice; and, therefore, that the limit of education ought not be assimilated to the limit of convention.

Cavell states that the rules do not tell us how to do the action well (unless 'well' is identified with intelligent action), because within the context of a statement of rules, doing it well is "doing it at all"—it is accomplishing the action technically, i.e., intelligently, in the way it *must* be done. While an action can be done poorly, such a case would occur when it is assessed vis- . à-vis the standard of what it is to do the action at all (what must be done) and so, if the actor can—at worst—be charged with deviating (with doing the action poorly), this only means that "poor" or "bad" refers to that which is not enforceably intelligible. It is equated with doing something in a way that is not recognizable as the action "at all."

Such a focus upon rules equates success and failure with enforceable conventions for deciding what is normal and what is deviant: "good" becomes equivalent to the power and clarity of intelligibility, and "bad" becomes that which is enforceably recognized as unintelligible.

Cavell misleads us into equating rule and principle with "must" and "ought," as if intelligibility is a sheer technical matter. In this case, our self-reflection upon our actions is completed when we see it with respect to its technical limitations as given by our construal of what the action is. Cavell understands the whatness of the action (what it is) as divided into two parts—what is necessary *that* it occur (rule) and given that it occurs, some additional notion of how its occurrence can be done well (principle). By separating "ought" from "must," he actually invests the action's sheer technical accomplishment (how it must be done) with principle by saying that *we ought to treat* the whatness of the action as how it must be done. But his sense of how it must be done is thoroughly technical. How the action must be done (to be done at all, to de done well) in his usage equates the principle of the action with competence, thus obscuring the essential notion of principle as origin (*arché*), as the need to undertake the action.

Perhaps the sense of principle we are developing is obscured in conventional formulations of the principled character of social action, because the origin of action in the deep need to undertake it in the first place is assumed to be shrouded in privacy. If, as Aristotle says, every action aims at some end, we suppose him to mean that every action is principled, that its being done shows an interest in wanting to do it. The actor does not act under the auspices of technical standards (such as what it is to *do* it); instead, he is guided by the standard of undertaking it, so that the need to undertake it becomes the standard of the action.

What is oriented to is not *techné* but the *desirable need* to do, which is to say that the oriented actor orients in the deepest sense to the desirable need to do whatever he is formulated as doing. To say that we understand the actor as affirming the worthiness of the action in his very doing of it, is to say that we see the action as making a statement that it is worth doing—that it *needs* to be done and this need is *desirable* A worthy action is not one that incidentally needs to be done (e.g., for personal or private reasons that are incidental to the action, or because the actor prefers to do it or chooses to do it); rather, it needs to be done because of its excellence. Any action is a sign (in de Saussure's sense) of excellence, a representation of the way in which community invests value in the structure of the world. A principled actor orients to the (essential) significance of his action in that he understands its being undertaken as a sign of value. A competent actor, in contrast, orients to the intelligibility of what he does, not to its significance, because for him that it is intelligible means that it is significant.

Thus, the principled actor does not act under the auspices of the nature (the whatness) of the action, because that whatness is only the representation of the action he creates for himself as its sign *given* his decision to undertake it. While some sense of what it is is prefigured in that decision, the election itself is accomplished as a feature of a reflection upon its doing as something that needs being done. This need, which is theorized as a feature of undertaking the action, is not reproduced by the representation of its whatness in the sign, for it evolves on the ground of a reflection upon the excellence of actions and so of the worthiness of undertaking the particular action.

In a related way, ends should be distinguished from intentions or goals, because ends reference the limits of an action as that where it ceases to be what is unlike it; intention or goal is merely the expression of that which is already undertaken. To accomplish the action is to undertake to care for or to nurture its development as a realization of the value or excellence that it signifies. We must be careful not to think of the end of the action as the skill or competence with which it is done, because that only sustains the distinction between facts and values. To undertake the action is to want to care for it as an expression of its limit as that realization of excellence (*areté*) it signifies.

We read the Greek notion of *areté* as referring not to the highest reaches of technical skill but, rather, to the idea of the worthiness of an action (an action, of course, conceived in its strict and strongest sense) as the difference that would be made between its being undertaken or not. That a difference would be made testifies to the excellence of the action.

An excellent action must be originated and sustained because it is one of the ways in which a community's conception of itself can be represented in a sign. In this way, we can imagine how wanting to undertake an action is wanting to undertake representing in action a sign of what the community needs and values, and so requires the actor's sense of the communal character of what is undertaken. To theorize undertaking is to reflect upon the quality or value of the action by asking how its being done signifies what is worth doing. Any action that is undertaken ought to make reference as its highest possibility to the way in which it signifies that actor's self-reflection upon how it represents the excellence for which it is intended to stand.

The actor oriented to either principle or rule orients to the need to be oriented. To say that an actor is oriented is then to say that he knows (that he is oriented to) *that he needs to be oriented.* Whether for rule or principle, the oriented actor is always oriented to desirable need (to the need to desire to be oriented). Such an actor is not merely "conscious of the fact" *that* he is oriented (which would only characterize his orientation empirically); rather, he recognizes as (the whatness) *what* his need is, the desirable need to be oriented.

The oriented actor who lives by convention (rule) identifies the need to be oriented as the need to be communicative and so as the need to orient to intelligibility, e.g., his concern with how intelligibility must be done at all to be done well. The rule-oriented actor accepts as his limit the concern with how the convention is done when it is done at all, and how it is done when it is done well.

The oriented actor who lives by principle identifies the need to be oriented as the need to theorize undertaking and so as the need to orient to the question of whether the particular convention—say, doing intelligibility— needs to be done, regardless of how it is done or how to do it well. *He then needs to orient to the need to orient to the question* (and he knows that he needs this) *of whether the convention is worth doing,* and so of whether he wants to do it. Of course, we are using "want" in a deep (and analytic) sense, not as a mere preference or compulsion. The principle-oriented actor accepts as his limit the need to orient to the convention as a sign of excellence, the need to recollect the convention as necessary and desirable.

In terms of the issues discussed in this monograph, the strongest oriented actor that we can envisage is not merely aware that he is oriented, but is oriented to the question of *what* he needs to be oriented to as a desirable need. If what he needs to be oriented to is the determinant sense of value attached to different actions as their ends or respective excellences, then the whatness to which he needs be oriented is the whatness expressed by excellence (not technical excellence, but the excellence that inheres in the world as a feature of the differences among human actions).

There is a difference between the action oriented to rule and intelligibility and the action oriented to principle and significance. For the former, the standard of reflective adequacy is mathematical in the original Greek sense of *mathesis*: self-reflection upon the rules underlying social action. While we agree that the oriented character of action always creates and presupposes an opportunity for the recollection of its rules, we can see that there are those who follow the rules unaware and so with no deep need to recollect (the many), and those who explicitly seek to define or formulate the rules (the few). Yet, neither of these has the need to give an account of— to orient to—the excellence of the rules. This excellence or principle cannot itself be laid down as another rule—its intelligibility is not enforceable— and yet it is the vivid origin of every human action.

If moral action makes reference to the best we can expect, it would take place as a discourse between teachers and those who are assumed to be in position to orient to what is needed (to principle, to excellence). Being in such a position presupposes skill, competence, and intelligence; it presupposes that they can be spoken in enforceably intelligible ways. But if this were the limit of moral education, *its* own excellence (the excellence of moral education) as an action would be limited to merely reinforcing resourceful competence in a population of apprentices. Rather, the student has to be in position to risk enforceable intelligibility (convention) itself in order to orient to excellence as what is needed and desirable.

NOTES

1. These are intended not to be behaviorally or logically inclusive but, rather, to stimulate examination of the nature of oriented action.

2. Cavell, *Must We Mean What We Say* (New York: Scribner's 1969), pp. 27-29.

3. Or—comfortably—both. But if that is comforting, it is because they do come together at times, when we knew they might not have; the actor can theorize the difference. When they do not come together, any decision is equally decisive, because the actor who knows this also knows he is an agent of the decision that presents and reaffirms the difference. If, as has been said, sanity is the moral alternative of our times, it is perhaps because the difference is now omnirelevant and always problematic.

Rules and Principles

We have attempted to depict the nature of self-reflection and of the self-reflective actor as one of principled speech, and we have had to construct such an actor by distinguishing him from one who is only a rule-guided speaker.

The difference between the principled speaker and the rule-guided speaker is difficult to grasp; indeed, it is the very difference between them that makes it so, since a rule cannot be consulted to resolve the difficulty. The selfsame speech you now read, for example, reflects this difference as the authorial ground of our work, work that is principled in the sense that we know we cannot give a rule for reading the difference, and yet we expect that the difference will be grasped in the reading and that its work as principled speech will become accessible as the ground of our usage.

In the *Moral Judgment of the Child,* Piaget provides an example that demonstrates the difference between rule and principle when he speaks of his daughter Jacqueline's understanding of rules.

Jacqueline has never been punished in the strict sense of the term. At the worst when she makes a scene, we leave her alone for a little while and tell her we shall come back when she can talk quietly again. She has never been given duties as such, nor have we ever demanded from her that sort of passive obedience without discussion which in the eyes of so many parents constitutes the highest virtue. We have always tried to make her understand the "why" of orders instead of laying down "categorical" rules. Above all, we have always put things to her in the light of cooperation: "to help mummy," "to please" her parents, to "show her sister" etc.,— are her reasons for carrying out orders that cannot be understood in themselves. As to rules that are unintelligible to very little children, such as the rule of truthfulness, she has never even heart mention of them.[1]

The idea that rules are unintelligible "to very little children," or that orders "cannot be understood in themselves" trades off the notion that children cannot comprehend the need for, and hence the principled character of, the rule.[2] For example, the rule of truthfulness is unintelligible only insofar as the spirit with which it must be invested by the one who submits to it—the necessity that it expresses—is not intelligible. But the child can certainly "understand" the practice to which the rule points as sheer behavior—in this example, not to soil the towel with dirty hands. If, from this perspective, rules *are* intelligible, from the perspective of their need or point or value, they are unintelligible. Thus, it is not that the child cannot comprehend rule, but that she cannot comprehend the idea of necessity, or of "point," or of value. Piaget confirms this when he continues "but in ordinary life it is impossible to avoid certain injunctions of which the purport does not immediately seem to have any sense from the child's point of view."[3]

Insofar as injunctions merely describe practices, they constitute no problem; yet, a spirited relationship to the injunction requires that we appreciate its point or purpose. If Piaget says that it is impossible to avoid injunctions that are incomprehensible, we might add that such incomprehensibility does not pertain to the technical character of the injunction but to its ground or reason. The deep sense of any order depends for its support upon an ascription of necessity without which the order is sheer *techné*. Piaget shows us through Jacqueline that the inability to understand an injunction is a feature of the failure to grasp the idea of the necessity of the practice. To understand an injunction in any but a technical way requires an understanding of various deep notions of moral requiredness, which the child does not grasp. The development of a strong rather than technical relation to the injunction requires a mastery of the very language that is at stake as a language that differentiates rule and principle. Inasmuch as the injunction always points to an action the mechanics of which—as action—can be grasped, it constitutes no problem; but the need for the action—the reason that conveys its necessity—is a tacit but essential feature of this very action. There is nothing in the injunction or in the action itself that recommends its necessity; thus, explanations that enumerate other reasons merely conceal the necessity for the action.

This sense of necessity that we seek to develop here depends upon a spirited assent to the convention itself as an action that *must* be done. The rule does not depend upon other rules; it depends upon the need to submit to the rule as a rule that is needed. If we say that the rule needs something other than itself, we only mean that it needs support in the form of spirited assent to it as good. Children can grasp rules; what they do not understand is how a rule requires something other than itself in the form of the support of spirited assent.

And we might ask, What grounds spirited assent? Rules must come to an end. At the base of life is the spirited assent we think of as principled commitment. What is unintelligible to the child is the way in which rule depends upon the particularity of such support.

Piaget's worry is this: Injunctions need to be supported by reasoning, because in the absence of explanations, the injunction appears arbitrary, and the child will develop bad habits of relating to authority externally or mechanically. Conversely, the child cannot understand the sense of commitment (the thoughtful submission) that the act of belief (and hence, the force of the injunction) requires. Piaget's solution is to make the injunction credible by enumerating other accounts or explanations (which are, in effect, other conventions) ad infinitum.

Piaget is responsive to the natural weakness of the child as one who cannot see the good of rule. This means that the child cannot yet appreciate the way in which necessity is established as an integral part of life. Basically, the child is too mechanical. Piaget desires to make the good of the rule comprehensible; yet, because of the child's essential limitation, Piaget can only enjoin the child to follow the rule or enumerate other rules mechanically, thus begging the question of *their* good. The mechanical injunction teaches that rules are binding because they exist (because they are enforceable, sanctioned). The arbitrary nature of rule by rule leaves its good in the hands of accident, for the child is bound by stipulation, by the stipulation that the rule must guide because it is enumerable. Though the convention could be otherwise, things nevertheless are the way they are, and we are bound to this; we must believe in the ways things are because that is the way they are. When rules bind in the absence of spirited assent, significance of an action is made identical with force, the need of the rule with the distribution of practical power, and the good of a practice with its intelligibility as a rule.

Above all we have always put things to her in the light of cooperation: "to help mummy."

The good of following the rule is to give mother pleasure, since soiling the towel displeases her. The good of the rule is discussed by invoking another rule—that it is good to give mother pleasure—the good of which is similarly unanalyzed. Piaget replaces one convention (soiling the towel) with another (the desire to gain mummy's affection).

It is not that Jacqueline should be disinterested in mummy's affection; rather, one needs to formulate the relation between soiling the towel and mummy's affection as an instance of the relation between convention and enjoyment. The injunction alone, the convention, would produce a mechanical attachment, not only to mummy but to convention; since a mechanical actor can only view himself as another condition, he is unable to review himself as one who is able to commit his self in a principled way, because convention can always be otherwise. And it is this that would be virtual disinterest, because, whatever one did, one would be doing it passively, out of compliance with the ecology of agreements. In this respect, if it is only a rule to satisfy mummy's preference not to soil the towel, then Jacqueline's interest in satisfying her is a matter of force—a matter of conditional affection—in which cooperation and enjoyment are seen as two conventions, each conditional upon the other.

In other words, to satisfy mummy's "preference" in order to gain her affection will guarantee an instrumental relation to convention (a conventional relation to convention), unless the knowledge that another's preference may be satisfied is itself seen as offering the engaged spirit of enjoyment. Presumably, Piaget wants to say that cooperation needs to be enjoyed, and so helping mummy is not the mean economy of mutually implicated pleasures received from satisfactions given, as though one's interest in enjoyment is conditional upon the independent satisfaction of a rule. Enjoyment is not just another convention when it is seen that cooperation needs to be enjoyed, and when this difference is understood as that between what could be otherwise (we may or may not cooperate) and what is necessary.

We must understand that the rule that guides us to avoid soiling the towel is not good because it gives mother pleasure, for this is as external to the rule's need as mentioning the number of people who would refuse to soil their towels. That following the rule gives mummy pleasure or coheres with the practices of most only makes the rule good by implication, that is, it is not good in itself but only in relation to some external rule.

Piaget teaches respect for the rule by using the child's respect for her mother. In this way, he makes the rule intelligible for the child by citing consequences or effects of not following it.

We have said that conventions are senseless when looked at by the child because they seem not to be self-justifying; they seem to be always in need of something other. To Piaget, the problem of preserving respect for the convention appears to depend upon providing credible explanations for them. Yet, such an explanation only externalizes the child's relationship to the rule, because it treats the convention as if it is good by implication (vis-à-vis its relation to something else) rather than in itself. To put it bluntly: *The child's unqualifiedness means that she cannot understand the conception of something as good in itself and the need to invest convention with necessity.* Instead of trying to teach *this,* Piaget transmits to the child a watered-down version of the Good as what is good by implication, i.e., as the valid.

Generally, then, when rules bind, they leave no room for principled interest because they survive in—and perhaps through—the absence of spirit; when principles are preferences, they leave no room for the essential, because they turn necessity into discretion. Each conception requires a mechanical actor in the sense that the need for rule becomes the limit, and so the best that can be done is to copy, discover, or construct the rule. Piaget's trouble surely is not this, for he could simply await the growth of enough "intelligence" or "competence" for Jacqueline to copy, discover, and construct. Rather, his trouble resides in the necessity that our need for rule is not exhaustive of our need; that a rule can be viewed as needing another, another that is not another rule. In effect, the mechanical actor assimilates his self to rule. The mechanical actor thus can never be decisive about rule because he is never given the opportunity to address the difference. Being unable to address the difference, he can never see the integration of rule and principle as a problem.

So, we need to understand the way in which the desire to please mother could be introduced not as another convention but as way of thinking strongly about what the child needs to do in the best sense. Can we then begin to think of the need to please mother not as something instrumental but as a necessity of the child as a child?

If we assume the parent as a good influence—which we must—then the mother's pleasure is grounded in the child's doing what is right. The mother's pleasure is grounded in the child's attempt to invest the convention with spirit as an attempt that the mother herself invites and seeks to influence. The mother embodies a spirited relation to the convention and is pleased only as the child strives to emulate her, even though the point of the convention is not grasped.

If the mother wants to teach the child what it is to choose a convention, this first requires compelling the child to accept the convention only because the adult's acceptance is spirited. The adult convinces the child that she is not ready to question the convention and that the parent's commitment can be trusted. The mother then gets pleasure when the child treats herself in the way in which the mother does, when the child imitates the mother's attitude toward the child by acting as if she (the child) assents spiritedly to the convention.

The child then needs to see *that* the parent is committed and how this shows in the parental acceptance of agreements. If the child copies the parent's acceptance of the convention, it is only because the child imitates the parent's commitment through the need to invest convention with spirit. In this way, the child learns the need of convention for passion.

If the parent is interested in the child's acceptance of convention, this is because the parent is spirited toward the convention and not just personal toward the child. The parent's interest in the child's relation to the convention ("don't soil the towel") should become an occasion for the child to develop interest in this relationship. If it is important to imitate the parent because what she does is right, this can only be done by imitating her. The question of a child is whether I should imitate because of *what* you are doing or because *you* are doing it. Pleasing the mother says, Accept that it is right because I am doing it until you can decide this question for yourself, the question of whether *what* I am doing is right.

Opinion and Knowledge

The course of action we have called self-reflection—the self-reflective actor—has necessarily been construed as oriented by some conception of its action as what self-reflection *is*. The traditional discussion of self-reflection, whatever the particular face ("knowledge," i.e., the knower; "wisdom," i.e., the wise man; "philosophy," i.e., the philosopher; "truth," i.e., the true speaker; etc.), has identified the self-reflective actor as the speaker who *must* proceed under the auspices of a certain conception of what he is doing (knowledge, wisdom, philosophy, truth). These auspices orient the speaker as to what it is to do what he does in the way it must be done (in the way it is right to do it). We read the various usages of the tradition as identifying that with which the course of action called self-reflection (or knowledge, wisdom, philosophy, truth . . .) has to be endowed—its parameters, its analytic character—in order to be adequately formulated as what it is.

Resistance to a conception of principled action as a difference from rule-guided action, in kind and not merely in degree, would lead to an understanding of our writing as redundant upon the dominant historic conceptions of self-reflection, which identify their ideal speaker as rule-guided. So we need to clarify the distinction between rule and principle by relating it to the tradition that shapes it, which contrasts with the purely rule-guided conception that pervades historic and recent examinations of social action. In order to understand our reading, one must see that we are using as a resource the very distinction between rule and principle that we want to elucidate, because we must read the tradition as if *it* is speaking in a principled way about self-reflection (this is our principle).

We think of the distinction of principle and rule as distinguishing two ideal speakers in a way that references the Platonic contrast between right judgment (true opinion, true belief) and knowledge (a distinction mentioned variously in the *Meno,* the *Theaetetus,* and *The Republic*). If the rule-guided speaker is similar to our (modern) conception of what Socrates meant by correct judgment, etc., and the principled speaker references our conception of the knower, then the self-reflective actor must be (endowed by us as) faithful to principle rather than to rule, if he is to be correct in a way that is other than accidental or conventional. The self-reflective actor has to be more than an interpreter or someone who applies rules correctly; a knower must be formulated as one who orients to the necessity of what is done, thus, as one who orients to the necessity of addressing necessity. What is necessary and desirable for the knower is that he accept the need and desirability to demonstrate the difference between what appears to be and what is, where that need is unshakable by persuasion. It is the very unshakability of this acceptance that empowers the knower to desire discourse that will demonstrate the difference in the case of the particular notion.

For example, in the *Timaeus,* the existence of the forms is said to follow from this distinction. Knowledge is produced by instruction, it is always accompanied by a true account of its grounds, it is unshakable by persuasion, etc. It is said that the slave in the *Meno* has a true belief until he can take himself through all the steps of the demonstration in order to see for himself with unshakable conviction that the proof is true. In some essential sense, "knowledge" assumes an actor who is oriented to the necessity of demonstrating or of persuading his self, one who needs to take his self through the steps, and so it assumes the knower as an actor who is unshakable in his conviction that *this* is what is needed. What the knower is unshakable about, then, is the need to orient to being unshakable as an end and limit. It is not the knower's opinion that is unshakable, it is his acceptance of the need for demonstration as necessary and desirable.

The "state of mind" of one who has knowledge (in the Socratic idiom) references the analytic requirements for our use of (the notion of) "knowledge." According to the dialogues, such a one needs to be construed as having assured himself through a reflection upon the grounds of his beliefs: Such assurance takes the form of being able to proceed through all the steps of the proof so as to establish for his self his unshakable conviction that the proof is true.

In other words, what we call knowledge (or any of its surrogates) is the action performed by one who knows, by a knower. These actions are not exhausted in word or behavior, for a knower and a believer might say the same words (might do the same behavior, might have the same opinions). A knower as distinct from a believer (a knower in the strict sense of the word) needs to be envisaged as one who orients to the need for self-assurance, as one who orients to the need to demonstrate to and for his self the necessity— the unshakable character—of the conviction. The knower is then oriented to demonstration, conviction, and necessity with reference to his self. We say that he needs to persuade or convince his self.

To unshakably convince oneself requires that one orient to the difference between right opinion and knowledge as necessary, where by right opinion we now reference the speaker who, like Weber, would limit speech to enforceable social sanction, i.e., to right opinion alone. It is important that this difference can be seen as necessary rather than as another conventional distinction, for the latter would bring us back to Jacqueline and the arbitration of one opinion by another. This is to say that what one knows is that convention is not knowledge, however convention may be enforceable and however it may serve the various conditions of social interaction and speaking with others. What is unshakable—immune to shifts in the validity of opinion—*is that knowledge is not convention,* even as it may depend upon convention to show itself in real courses of action. The discrimination of knowledge as distinct from conventionally offered discretion is the knowledge shown in discriminating *that* difference.

If convention were the limit, there could be just two basic orders of behavior: acting correctly, enforceably, or acting incorrectly, unenforceably. Action could only be understood in terms of its competence, and it would either conform or deviate in any instance. Here, for example, the exclusively rule-guided actor is given no opportunity to affirm his deviance as an expression of the difference between rule and principle. If the revolutionary is the most committed deviant, he would in this sense be "committed" only to reconstituting one set of rules with another. He could only be characterized as one who fails to cooperate.

All this is precisely Jacqueline's condition, and Piaget's trouble, in that competence guides as rule guides, and so spirit is made identical to obligation. The *decisive* possibility of any relation between self and convention, as in the possibility that Jacqueline could enjoy cooperation, is made to disappear, because competence only reproduces the rule. The only problem for wise, true, philosophical, or knowing speakers would be to follow the opinion competently, to comply. Principle would be a danger here, because spirit can always violate obligation by reflecting the difference between what we know and the obligation to be correct. Knowledge, thus, is capable of doing violence to the ideal speaker of convention by reformulating what is required as the difference between that speaker (what is sanctioned) and principle (what is essential). The knowing speaker can review and recommit his self to that which is enforceable. The knowing speaker can be decisive about competence.

"Going through the steps," then, is neither the equivalent of socialization nor the instruction of oneself in the validity of correct opinion; rather, it is to establish for oneself the unshakable difference between knowledge and correctness. In this sense, the Socratic knower (our self-reflective actor) and the self-conscious man of Hegel's phenomenology are oriented in the same way: It is not that they are "subjective," "conscious," "intentional," etc., but that, oriented to the need to be oriented, they orient to the need to demonstrate (to collect) the necessity (collectedness) that constitutes one as a particular one, that collects speech as the collectedness that it is. They orient to what the person *as* a self-conscious speaker needs to orient to as his ground.

What this means is that a knower is not only oriented ("aware") but that he is oriented to the need to be oriented: The knower orients to the need to convince his self. That the knower can so orient means that the knower knows what knowledge is and what it is not. The knower acts under the auspices of the difference between knowledge and correct opinion, and so he exemplifies that his belief is chosen, i.e., (for the reason) because it is an example of what is good (of knowledge). The one with true belief does not provide for the choiceworthiness of his belief. Both might be correct in that they affirm the same opinion, but the knower is (assumed to be) required to orient to what he affirms as different from what is excluded, because it does not resemble knowledge but *is* knowledge. What the knower knows, then, is not any particular opinion but the way in which any particular affirmation acquires its status as knowledge, because its character as knowledge is demonstrated in discourse.

In the Socratic tradition, the self-reflective actor—the one who knows—
is not one who happens to be correct but is the one who knows what knowing
is and whose knowing what knowing is is exemplified in any particular
opinion that he happens to have. In other words, it is not the particularity of
the opinion that makes one the knower, it is the analytic requirement that we
ascribe to him as an actor who exemplifies knowing. In this tradition, to say
of someone that he is a knower is not to say that he is oriented or that he
knows something in the way in which we know that Montreal is north of
Toronto (much discussion of the self-reflective actor and of knowledge uses
this version of knowledge as its resource); it is to say that a knower is one
who knows what knowing is and (so) what it is not and who orients to, and
acts under, the auspices of this distinction.

In this sense, the one who knows that Montreal is north of Toronto has
right judgment, correct opinion, or true belief but not necessarily knowledge,
unless we can ascribe to him (to this opinion) its exemplary status as an
instance of knowledge. Although this opinion is affirmed through the application of some rule to the facts, in what it affirms it does not in itself provide
for the need to undertake being ruled by the rule; the self-conscious actor
does not merely use the usage (he does not merely apply the rule of
geography), but he also needs to be conceived as having a duty to the usage
(to the rule). One who is formulated as having a duty to the rule of usage
must be understood as drawing upon more than rule or usage, since the
spirited assent entails no particular usage (unless we formulate it statistically).
The question is: How can one be formulated as dutiful in a spiritual way to
the opinion in the correct judgment?

In the correct opinion that Montreal is north of Toronto, we do not have
knowledge. The quest to determine how this can be said asks us to specify
the analytic requirements of the self-conscious actor as the requirements
with which we need to endow the speaker (whatever the particular usage), in
contrast to the typical actor, for correct judgment.

If we treat the opinion (that Montreal is . . .) as a terminal state of affairs
or as an accomplishment of an unknown course of action, we understand its
sense to be decidable in alternative ways. In this vein, we envisage the one
who opines as using methods and procedures that are designed to make the
opinion happen. By conceptualizing the user as one who uses (whatever)
methods to make the opinion happen, we conceive of the task of theory to be
one of supplying the account (rules, machinery, the logos) that the user must
employ in order to produce the opinion.

Because the actor is guided by the usage, the limits of his environment of
knowledge (the limits of the knowledge ascribed to him by the theorist) must

be drawn around some version of rules for identifying and interrelating places and distances, etc. Such a skillful actor is not necessarily self-conscious. In the first place, his so-called knowledge occurs because he conforms to a standard that enforces the adequacy of the rules he uses. The Montreal-Toronto opinion, for example, suggests some notion of a common measure, in which correct opinion is what is typical. While these rules of calculation are assumed to be good (they get him from one place to the other, etc.), the need they reflect is not addressed as a feature of what he knows. What he could know here, say, is the need and not just the skill to speak as another would—that is, to speak in common by measuring one's own speech against its reproducibility in another.

This means, secondly, that the knower must be guided by more than rules or usage (because rules/usage is not knowledge). Of course, deeply, one governed by conventions has submitted to the principle of the binding and valid character of rules/usage, but that submission is not reflective unless it shows an orientation to the difference between what it affirms and what it denies as a difference that is necessary, a difference that is good. The Montreal-Toronto opinion is not autobiography, because in this formulation geography will not be made to happen except as it is common. What is important about commonly reproducible speech? Why do we need it? Simply to cite the social order problem, which common speech is often said to solve, hardly addresses its necessity as that to which we ought orient.

That the knower orients to demonstration means that he treats the Montreal-Toronto opinion as speech that raises the question of the difference between what resembles a true speech and what *is* a true speech. In this sense, the difference between certainty and truth is raised, for while the opinion is held with assurance, in order for the notion (e.g., knowledge) to have its essential and implicit nature developed in discourse, the knower must demonstrate how assurance is not essential to what a strong conception of knowledge *is* (though it *appears* to be).[4]

The exemplary ideal actor for "knowledge" construed by various intellectual traditions in epistemology, the philosophy of science, logic and the sociology of knowledge has never attempted to provide for such requirements, presumably because they have treated knowledge technically as a species of intelligence or competence, i.e., as a kind of skill or faculty. Within these traditions, those who rebel through their various post-Wittgensteinian recognitions that rules do not cover all contingencies cannot imagine a positive version of a knower as anything more than a conventionalist or an anarchist. In this move, of course, they show that they cannot conceive of positive alternatives to a rule-governed world; that they are unable to reachieve the Greek conception of principle (of commitment) as something other than rule means that they will produce deviation from rule as the only intelligible alternative.

In contrast, for us the self-conscious actor needs to be construed as guided by Desire; in this way, the opinion—the usage—is a medium through which he expresses Desire. The self-conscious actor needs to be seen as guided not by usage/rules but by the need (Desire) to say something other than what can be said (other than usage). We see the usage that is taken as the terminal point and the limit in most versions of knowledge as the *metaphor* through which Desire inscribes itself in practice.

The question for our theorizing is then different. In the former case, the theorist asks for the account that will provide the usage with its sense (its intelligibility), as the account that could be seen to be employed by the user in order to accomplish what he does. In our case, the theorist asks for the Desire for which the usage substitutes, by seeking to reachieve in a narrative a conversation among the different senses that coexist in language as Desire, need, duty, obligation, preference, value, etc. In this case, the theorist formulates an actor who achieves the usage (that Montreal is north of Toronto) as an intended solution to the problem of Desire (of need, duty), as one who is self-conscious (who orients to the difference between usage and other) when particular usage is an intended solution to the problem of the self-conscious actor. Whereas what the Montreal-Toronto opinion affirms could be shaken by persuasion (imagine a southern city being named or renamed Montreal), it is not imaginable that the need for demonstration could be so overturned as long as we live discursively.

The Principled Actor

Our emphasis on the distinction between rule and principle is intended to show the problem of conceiving of the social actor as if he is exclusively rule-guided. We have not been saying that the principled actor has no place for rule, because we know that any principled relationship to speech needs to treat various agreements as acceptable-without-question in order to survive.

To recapitulate the contention of this work: We have said that the theorist needs to be conceived as a principled actor, and we have examined certain resonances of that proposition.

That the proposition itself affirms a principle suggests one feature of principled action: Since it is originally and essentially social, we can appreciate the problem of any version of conduct that requires as an ideal speaker one detached from any end. Principled action always begins *en medias res.*

Further, if the intelligibility of our proposition depends upon the accessibility of the distinction between rule and principle, in stating the proposition we use that to which it refers as a resource. We use the very distinction we make in order to make the distinction. This tells us something else about principled action in that the actor acts upon the basis of some agreement concerning action itself.

What he proposes is already a part of what he is proposing. This is to say that he uses his sense of what is needed in a way that cannot be enforceably justified through an appeal to everything other than the authority of his own particularity. But neither of these features differentiates principled action from any instance of interpretive competence.

To say one is principled is to say that one needs to act out of a sense of need—of necessity—which is not covered by any explicit agreement about what is to be (what needs to be) done. We say that such an actor exhibits the risk that is a feature of any authoritative social action. The social actor is always conceived as one who organizes his action as a particular solution to the problem of what needs to be done, because the solution to that problem is always and essentially particular, since it always and essentially presupposes (uses) the resourcefulness of *any* agreement it accepts.

As the principled actor (as theorist) is a personification of our understanding of the social actor in the highest sense, what we say of principled action holds for social action. In this way, we begin to provide for what is quintessentially social about action.

We see that social action is not sufficiently formulated when it is characterized as subjective, oriented . . . etc., because such designations characterize any rule-guided or competent action. All such designations say is that social action must be, at minimum, a species of conventional action. This is a nice reminder, if it does not confuse a condition with what is essential. What is essential in this instance is that the principled actor knows his commitment is a self-sanctioning need in the sense that it cannot be accounted for in terms of the conditions under which it arises. Although principle can be made subject to history—to conditions—this would not be a principled understanding of principle. That social action is committed to the necessity of its commitment means that the original relationship for social action, and hence the original social relationship, is between the actor and his environment of needs. The identity and difference of this relationship is that the environment is both internal and external. The social actor must be seen as originally and essentially guided by needs whose intelligibility, clarity, and weight depend upon him and him alone, in the sense that any and all appeal to the rule (to agreement, to convention) to establish intelligibility, clarity, and weight is, as an appeal, always referencing something deeper than a rule—it is an acknowledgment of need. Of course, such an acknowledgment *can be read* as a self-description of rule (of the acceptance of an agreement, of a convention), but such acceptance only testifies to the need for the rule of accepting what is acceptable as a rule that is needed deeply.

The social actor is paradoxical in the sense that what he depends upon, *he* produces. His very activity both testifies to the power of what he needs and qualifies that power in this very testimony. That is, he makes it what it is, yet he can only do this while being in the grip of what he makes. If the power of the needs that guide the actor were unqualified, the actor would be social in a weak sense. He would be mechanical or rule-governed in that he would be one who just applies what is first given. While such a competent actor often appears to be social, we are saying that his particularity does not have sufficient strength to do more than serve as a vehicle for the "interpretive" application of rules to situation. He is mechanical because he is not constructed as one who applies the rule as a decisive display of his own particularity, and so he is not one who orients to integration of the external (rule) and the internal (his self) as itself the problem to which he attends. The mechanical actor lacks spirit, because the way he is constructed gives him no opportunity to integrate (or not) rule and self. He either follows or he doesn't. In the latter instance, he can only be deviant; he is not endowed with any capacity to elect not to follow for a good reason that could be more than an excuse, more than a citation of special conditions that all (could) agree to have kept him from following. This mechanical actor is given the chance to fail the rule, then, but not to resist it except by reference to another rule, to another condition.

We start with a conception of a social actor whose interest is to supply competence with spirit in the sense that his sociality includes a deeper sense of what accepting an agreement or rule is than is usually provided in discussions of rule. The principled actor accepts the need of an agreement for the spirit that invests the agreement with a sense of its necessity. What the principled actor accepts, then, is that rules are not self-justifying and self-certifying, which means that he accepts the need of any convention for something other than itself in order to be convincing. Conviction requires supplying the convention with a spirited submission to its acceptability on the grounds of the need of life for the convention. The principled actor is not one who seeks on every actual occasion simply to produce union between self and rule, for this would be to treat the possibility of union as another rule or condition. Rather, *en medias res,* he seeks to sustain on every occasion the *problem* of the external and the internal. This is to say that what is unconditional about principle is that it always raises the question of the relation between self and rule as a necessary question. The principled actor questions (his own integration) unconditionally. His deepest failure would be to annihilate that question, whatever his failures of competence, errors of interpretation, or lowliness of spirit.

The distinction between rule and principle that we have advanced can be seen as a resource for addressing the question, What are our necessities? This question seeks to identify that to which social action as an ideal speaker is committed. The "necessities" of this (constructed) actor reference the limits or imperatives to which he is construed as needing to be oriented in order to realize his (analytic) character as "social." The conventions of philosophy and sociology speak of such necessities in terms of various notions such as expectation, obligation, right, exigency, and so forth.

In the strong sense, any conception of a social actor has to be constructed *as if* it is oriented in the strong sense, and so *as if it* is endowed with a sense of limit, imperative, and necessity. In this way, any actor is conceived as if he is an example of a strong conception and so, as if he is a strong social actor. For example, much work in ethics and in sociology is devoted to asking *if* we are obligated and how we discover answers to this question. Such work is not motivated by a principled sense of the necessity for inquiry to formulate a strong social actor, because limit is conceived to be entirely internal (subjective) or entirely external (obligatory). Generally, that work treats a principled conception of inquiry as subjective, dogmatic, etc., because it needs to think of any ascription of authority as by nature an attribution that is either discretionary or supported by nothing other than convention. The only agreement that can be accepted by such work is that there is nothing beyond agreement.

When we actually confront this discretionary-conventional actor, his alien nature is striking:

> I'd passed my life a certain way, and I might have passed it in a different way, if I'd felt like it. I'd acted thus, and I hadn't acted otherwise; I hadn't done x, whereas I had done y or z. . . . Nothing, nothing had the least importance . . . all the ideas that people had tried to foist on

me . . . What difference could they make to me, the deaths of others, or a mother's love, or . . . God; or the way a man decides to live, the fate he thinks he chooses, since one and the same fate was bound to "choose" not only me but thousands of millions . . . And what difference could it make if, after being charged with murder, he were executed because he didn't weep at his mother's funeral, since it all came to the same thing in the end?[5]

Although the estranged modern actor is typically thought to be the victim of anomie—of the absence or confusion of convention—we can see here quite another understanding: He is dispirited not because rules are absent but because they are present in the absence of principle ("Nothing, nothing had the least importance"). Nor is he unfamiliar with conventions ("I hadn't done x, whereas I had done y or z"); indeed, it is the case that conventions are all *too* familiar, they are invested with no necessity ("I might have passed it in a different way, if I'd felt like it"). There is nothing decisive about discretion in a world where all things could be otherwise, even as many can be observed to be doing the discretion that, convention calls for ("What difference could they make to me . . . the way a man decides to live?"). In this, the discretionary-conventional actor is a grown-up Jacqueline. He does not need another convention, he needs what could matter about convention, unless all is to "come to the same thing in the end."

On another occasion, this actor, whom we now reinvent as the best example of the social in modern theory, is sitting beside the body of his dead mother and wonders whether he should smoke:

. . . I wanted a cigarette. But I wasn't sure if I should smoke, under the circumstances—in Mother's presence. I thought it over; really, it didn't seem to matter, so I offered the keeper a cigarette, and we both smoked.[6]

Whether to smoke is likened to the multiplicity of opinion and does not provide a grip on things except as arbitrary: to smoke is to choose, not to smoke is to choose, and "It didn't seem to matter," not because opinion is unintelligible as a rule, but because the intelligibility of either choice cannot be infused with necessity.

We say this lack is not a contingency or exception but a theoretic requirement for all actors whose limits are constructed as the conventional and competent and agreeable. The languor of such an actor is a good example of modern theory, not a poor one, because one who is constructed to choose agreeably, without any sense of necessity, will never show spirit.

And this is a modern creation, because for moderns, our limits originate in the agreement to treat agreement as our limit.

Thus, the principled speaker risks humiliation when he is confronted with one who acts in accord with the ideal speaker constructed by modern theory. Humiliation is not the deep failure of failing to do what is right (failing to be principled, for example). Rather, the principled speaker risks that his commitment will be treated as discretionary or as conventional, and so that he will be treated as one who does not know that he does not know. He risks, then, having his commitment (his genuine ignorance in regard to the particularity of his requirements) treated as if it is a sign of his dogmatic, opinionated, capricious, and subjective character. Whereas real failure is failure to be moderate—failure to be reserved toward convention and ironic at being neither convention nor desire but needing both—humiliation is this moderation when it is seen as excess.

One way to understand the problem of inquiry into our necessities is through an appreciation of its character as a search for rules to decide which behavior needs to be done. In this foreshortened view, we discover that to which we are committed—what we need to do—by discovering the rules that provide with complete and enforceable clarity for what we are to do. The problem of the principled actor's commitment to necessity is now transformed to exemplify the case of the competent actor's obligation to rule.

By now, however, many have come to accept the notion that the necessities of a speaker are not circumscribed by rules, because language needs to be conceived as more than a collection of rules, and necessity always points to the problem of moral (i.e., excellent) speech. Any conception of language as a system of rules (as conventions, agreements about how we speak) still lacks spirit. In other words, the way in which these agreements need to be invested with the authority claimed for them is lacking in any formulation of the agreements as self-sufficient according to rule.

While many have recognized this sense of the so-called incompleteness of rules, the recognition has been handled in different ways. Some, for example, have cited it as proof of the *weakness* of rules, and so as grounds for skepticism about the possibility of strong speech. Either all speech is merely opinionated, or we should scale down our aspirations and speak only in a way that could satisfy clear and enforceable agreements about speaking procedure. These possibilities are anticipated in the concession that because rules are incomplete, discretion must be exercised even as one seeks to be guided by rule. However, if necessity is thought unable to survive the incompleteness of rule, this discretion will always appear arbitrary, because the weakness of rule would make its connection to any act a purely techical matter of clarifying opinion or adapting to that which is enforceable. We are thus back where we began: Rules are incomplete and call for discretion, but discretion conceived without principle leaves us without anything but (incomplete) *techné* or rule with which to grapple with the problem. The source of authority and stability in any orderly phenomenon is here provided through the sheer power (and so the discretion or conventionality or caprice) of the speaker to enforce his own solutions to incompleteness whenever the problem rises to the surface. There is in this version a reluctance to acknowledge both (1) that rules need something Other and (2) that the limit of a principled actor can include commitment. Accordingly, (1) is seen to make (2) impossible, because it is said that in the absence of rule the authority ascribed to action is discretionary in the weakest sense.

Others have conceded that rules are authoritative when weight is attributed to the discretions and agreements they offer. Such rules are said to be valid, which means they are endowed with authority by implication, by the stipulation that they are to be treated as such because they share some characteristic with others similarly treated. Notions such as "ought,' values, and goals are pertinent here, for they endow rules with authority by virtue of instrumental reasoning, which cites the consequences or effects of not following the rules, or which attributes authority to them by virtue of how they originate from the number of members who accept them.

In cases such as these, rules acquire confirmation through values that invest conventions with their moral authority. Those who accept such a position say that values cannot be binding in the way that rules supposedly are; they say that values cannot be justified as sources of commitment because they, too, are conventions, conventions that elicit a wider following. Since other reasonable conventions can be cited as reasons for accepting their authority because of what would happen in the absence of the acceptance of such rules, values, at best, are good only by implication. A value is good by implication in this weak sense when the demonstration of how it *is* good rather than apparently good is developed by enumerating negative consequences of its not being accepted or by citing the extent of its acceptance. A stronger notion of implication was developed by Socrates in the exchange with Thrasymachus, when he showed justice to be good by implication through his demonstration of how justice could not (essentially) be as it was reputed to be in various opinions. But here, as Glaucon pointed out, while he showed that justice was necessary through some vision of the limits necessary to form the opinions, it was not yet shown to be desirable in itself and thus remains good by implication.

In asking after our necessities, the principled speaker addresses the self as his topic because the necessities after which he quests are the imperatives for the ideal speaker. The ideal speaker is not a surrogate for any one particular individual, but is a personification of the realization of the social actor. The "self" is then, first, the self of the "we"—of man envisaged as idealization—rather than of the "me," and is, secondly, as an idealization, a formulation of desirable limits and essentials rather than of incidentals.

We say that it is the nature of the principled speaker to treat the question of the nature of the principled speaker—his desirable limits, necessities—as his problem. The question with which we endow the principled speaker is what founds and grounds the principled speaker? This rule allows us to relate to our material: By treating every practice and usage as if it is (principled) a text that is interested in being responsive to *that* question, we show our interest in exemplifying a responsiveness to that question.

Since inquiry is now understood as having an interest in laying the grounds for a treatment of human conduct as principled, it proceeds by asking (by formulating) wherein resides the particular strength—the particular imperative sense of limitation—of any practice. There is a difference between posing that question as if it is concerned to clarify the technical character of the practice and as if it is interested in formulating the imperativeness of the practice. The practice is understood in the first case when the strength of its commitment is seen as valid (as good by implication) rather than, as in the second case, good in itself (and so it is falsely understood when it is seen not as an icon of Desire for the good, but as an example of rule-guided behavior).

To reassert the identity of the principled and self-reflective actor: (1) it is an idealization rather than a description of (2) man rather than ego. This is the sense in which self is both a topic and a resource, because "self" is analytically understood as the necessities, limits, and imperatives of the human. The interchangeability of topic and resource means only that being human is to ask after the foundation of the human. To ask after the human is to exemplify the human, since the human is part of the whole. Inquiry is the way in which the human exists as such a part by asking after the relationship of part to whole.

The tradition that called Socrates the founder of the study of self-reflection is confirmed in the description of Socrates as one who turned us away from curiosity about the cosmos and toward the study of man. This association identifies self-reflection with the study of what is familiar and treats the familiar as the self. In other words, self-reflection is the study of the familiar, now understood as the study of man. Self-reflection as the reflection upon the self is intelligible as a reflection upon the limits of the "we." What is most interesting about the tradition of self-reflection that Socrates originated is that the familiar is engaged with spirit only by reserving the temptation to surrender to familiarity in order to ask with strength after what is essential and necessary.

Socrates taught us that this self-reflection cannot be divined if it is understood as an interaction: He suggested that the relation between reflection and the self upon which it reflects can only be captured by figures of speech that evoke in extraordinary ways the need to undertake the action: Desire, recollection, passion, wonder. The practices of such an actor (the theorist) have been described in a tradition as ironic questioning. This is to say that a principled relation to knowledge is essentially ironic and is depicted in the figure of the actor who relates with confidence to the whole, and so to the problem of the place of man (of discourse) within the whole.

Irony: the Way of Life of the Principled Actor

Imagine now the theoretic man as the one exercised and animated by the problem of knowledge, i.e., by the problem of the desirable necessity of theorizing. To this man, theorizing is a moral problem insofar as the issue of what it is to know (and so to not know) is a fundamental issue for him. In the language of Hegel, he is fired by the problem of knowledge, he is passionate toward it.

For any notion, we imagine and develop an actor who is construed as passionate toward the problem expressed by the notion; in Hegel's language, he is "subject to the concept and master of its use." In their various ways, such actors stand to their notions as surrogates for the theorist's relation to the notion of knowledge. Note that in Hegel we begin with the theorist's need for knowledge as a Desire to think the problem to its foundation; it is this Desire that produces, in its way, the theorist's continuous dissatisfaction.

A consequence of what we say here is that the problem posed by knowledge (and by any notion) is moral rather than technical (or even ethical). This means that the actor is reverent toward the necessity that inheres in the notion as its implicit and to-be-worked-out material. The confidence to accept the inescapable necessity of what is real is actually a recognition that frees him to act. In this respect, we might think of the theorist and his fate. Hegel suggests this fate as the capacity to act without division. We are laying the ground for irony as the capacity to act without being distracted by what (because of its necessity) needs to be suffered as real (inescapable) and, *because of this,* left behind. Since one can know only a part of all that is involved in action, one is responsible for everything, even what is beyond our control.

A feature of the commitment of the principled actor (in this case, the theorist) is that he speaks as a social being expressing a universal order (think of Hegel's example of Antigone). In this way, he orients to the order as binding and good and to his speech as the exemplification of a communal conception of excellence. We conceive of the principled actor as personifying a social necessity.

Our problem now is to demonstrate how we can develop a positive and enjoyable version of discourse as an ironic relation to language, and to do so by starting with a notion of the theorist as moral actor. Let us for this purpose begin with a maxim for this theorist and seek to develop *as he would* the necessity of irony from a consideration of the maxim.

Everything depends upon grasping and expressing the ultimate truth . . . as subject.[7]

As subject: to grasp and express the ultimate truth as subject to . . . ? To what is the ultimate truth subject? In order to grasp the ultimate truth as subject, we need to understand to *what* the ultimate truth is subject.

This much seems clear: If it is ultimate, the truth is subject to nothing. Yet, it has to be grasped and expressed, and so, in this respect, it is subject to the need to grasp and express, i.e., to discourse. We can appreciate the irony of: the ultimate truth is subject to discourse (its majesty must be adapted to human needs of grasping and expressing).

And, of course, discourse is subject to the "ultimate truth." Certainly, discourse is not king; it cannot be self-governing, and it cannot be unregulated by anything other.

When we say that discourse is subject to the ultimate truth, we mean that it is not free to speak about anything and everything but only about the ultimate truth. That is, if the ultimate truth must be accessible to discourse, discourse must have the power to distinguish what is incidental from what is ultimate.

In this sense, the great insight of theorizing is to affirm our need to live enjoyably with this irony: That the absolute character of the "ultimate truth" is denied by its dependency upon discourse and by the need to be grasped and expressed, and that the absolute character of discourse (of the speaker, of the ego) is denied by its being *en medias res.*

To understand the ultimate truth as subject to discourse and discourse as subject to the ultimate truth is to understand the ultimate truth as language and language as subject. Language is subject to the law of development which is the law of the whole, i.e. (all is one in development. In this respect, the self-development of the notion (of discourse reflecting upon itself) is the medium wherein theorizing exists.

The self-development of the notion means: Discourse needs to work itself out as its way of realizing (by making explicit) what implicitly (and essentially) belongs to it. The notion reflects into its own self as its way of theorizing itself. We say the notion "works itself out," it develops what it really is, it brings itself to itself. Thus, self-identity is the way in which the whole ("the ultimate truth," "what truly is") works itself out through discourse. This "working out" is the notion's self-development; it is its reflection into itself wherein it develops (works out and makes explicit) what essentially (and implicitly) belongs to it.

This is to say that the notion develops, works out, and makes explicit what necessarily belongs to it. Implicitly (and essentially) the notion is identical to itself—it cannot be unlike itself, because it must be limited by what is unlike it. It takes work to develop and make explicit the self-identity of the notion. This means that it takes work to make explicit what essentially belongs to the notion.

What essentially belongs to the notion is that which makes it what it is and not other to itself, that which makes it the same and not the other, that which announces its content as the particular notion that it is. A feature of its being itself—of what it *is*—is its not being the other; this is not a lack but part of its determination.

The character of the notion does not automatically develop; it has to be worked out in discourse. The theorist's labor is guided by the Desire to make explicit the developed and essential form of the notion. He does not have a particular image before his mind, but rather he recognizes the need to be guided by the needs of development (of working out).

To grasp the ultimate truth as subject is to grasp the principle of self-identity. What this means is that we need to grasp discourse as an instance of development.

What "develops" in discourse? Conversation "grasps and expresses" what belongs implicitly and essentially to the notion. Conversation itself "develops" by working out and making explicit how the content of the notion belongs to it by necessity.

The working out of this connection (of the notion to its own content) is a making explicit of the relation of notion to itself (self-identity) where what this working out anticipates must, in turn, first be "glimpsed" by the worker as a necessity for him and then "expressed" through his own labor, which aspires to determine (to give determination, content to) the notion.

The development of the notion must be worked out by a worker who will only undertake this project if he first grasps the need to express the ultimate truth as working itself out through the self-identify and self-development of the notion (of discourse) as a need that is truly necessary and not under his discretion to alter.

How does knowledge realize itself as knowledge? To ask this is to ask how knowledge realizes itself as other than nonknowledge? Nonknowledge is not the opposite of knowledge—as ignorance, for example—but is that which is other than knowledge (which could be everything). Thus, to ask "what is knowledge?" or "how does knowledge realize itself as knowledge?" is to raise the question of how knowledge is both (at the same time) the same (as itself) and other (than itself). To ask how knowledge realizes itself as knowledge (and so, as other than nonknowledge) is to ask after what belongs essentially to and with knowledge. This question presupposes the power to imagine something larger than knowledge, something like the "ultimate truth" or whole, which includes in its kin both knowledge and what is other than knowledge.

The power to imagine the whole is the power to imagine how knowledge exists as the same and the other; it is the power to imagine how the notion and what is other to it are part of the notion itself. Any grasp of knowledge, then, must express the distinction between what is knowledge and what is other than knowledge as a relationship *internal* to knowledge itself. Any cultivated notion of knowledge develops an argument on how knowledge develops from out of this relationship.

The comparison is not between knowledge and ignorance, because ignorance is not the other of knowledge but its opposite; what is other to knowledge is what *appears* to be knowledge. Discourse does its work by developing this difference as a difference given by the multitudinous uses of knowledge.

There are those who would identify knowledge in certain ways and let it go at that. They would not see knowledge as needing to express something essential, thus, as the working out of an argument; instead, they would be satisfied with being arbitrary about the content of knowledge. We want to say that the demand of self-identity that governs the development of the notion means that the notion works out and makes explicit the *necessity* of what belongs to it *vis-à-vis* the coincidence of what is other to it. The multitudinous uses of knowledge make a demand upon us to heed the need of knowledge (of the notion) to develop and make explicit what is implicit and essential.

If each notion can be understood as an argument, we might say that each notion makes a claim as to what it is, as to what is essential to it. Any version of knowledge that does not grasp and express the necessity in its development as a differentiation from what is other to it is not subject to the need to grasp and express the ultimate truth. The self-development of the notion is the way in which the ultimate truth develops and works itself out—it is the medium of the ultimate truth's existence; this is what is intended when it is said of the "ultimate truth" that it is "one principle taking shape in diverse ways."[8]

Can we say in the first instance, that the ironic interest is enlivened by the power to imagine the working out of self-identity as an unfolding of movement and development? Irony reacts to multiplicity and to its animation by grasping it, in the first instance, as the way in which the ultimate truth works itself out. "Movement" expresses the way in which the ultimate truth experiences its diversity and seeks to develop and work out what is necessary to its own multitudinousness. Uncollected movement *(multis)* is undisciplined before it has grasped the need to express its self-identity as a process of realizing and making explicit what belongs to it necessarily. Such a state perishes as uncollected movement desires to develop into what it implicitly is, as it aspires to take itself in hand.

In this way, the speaker himself works out his own self-identity through his development of what belongs to the notion. Through discourse, the speaker shows his interest in embodying the desire to work out and make explicit what *he* is.

Is this the material of irony, to know that in our development of the self-identity of the notion, at the same time we work out and make explicit the self-identity of man?

To grasp the ultimate truth as subject: to Desire to express the ultimate truth. Our Desire to grasp and express the ultimate truth is embodied in our need to work out the self-development of the notion.

The notion is not the ultimate truth, and the ultimate truth is not (merely) the most comprehensive notion.[9] Our interest in the ultimate truth is shown (indirectly) or is embodied in discourse as an interest in working out the development and self-identity of the notion. Our interest in the ultimate truth is in need of embodiment. It has to be worked out because it "exists" only at the level of discourse (at the level of the notion).

What is worked out by the theorist, then, is the development of the notion and not the development of the "absolute truth." If we laugh at the attempt to work out and make explicit the development of the absolute truth, we are only laughing at the confusion of principle with notion.

The ultimate truth works itself out as subject and is to be so grasped and expressed insofar as we work out and develop the self-identity of the notion.

To say that the theorist "suffers" the inescapable necessity of what is real, is to say that his interest is perfectly comfortable with this ironic relationship to the ultimate truth (that needs discourse) and to the notion (that needs the ultimate truth). Because the theoretic interest affirms that the ultimate truth is "one principle taking shape in diverse ways," it knows not only that the diverse ways are grounded in the ultimate truth, but that the ultimate exists in the diversity of *its* ways. The diverse ways through which the ultimate truth expresses itself are not ways external to the ultimate truth, but ways in which the ultimate truth is what it is.

The theoretical interest loves its fate in the sense that it is assured that it works out the development of the notion as a means of expressing the ultimate truth . . . "as subject." It does not feel as if it is consigned to inferior status because of this, or that it is related to the ultimate truth only instrumentally or abstractly. Its interest in the development of the notion— in the unfolding of its in-itself—is the way the human embodies its interest in expressing (the development and unfolding of) the ultimate truth as subject.

Let us suggest that our enjoyment depends upon the power to resist treating the ultimate truth as if it was another notion and that guilt only occurs when we suspect that we have assigned the ultimate truth a special place. We have been unfair to the notion! We have treated discourse as inferior vis-à-vis the ultimate truth! Our problem is to be comfortable with the special character of the ultimate truth.

We might imagine our limit (our flaw) to reside in our inability to express the ultimate truth directly; our fate is to be able to express it "only" by working out the development of the notion. Could we imagine this limit as other than a privation but as an incentive? The ironic interest starts with this: that it is necessary to be influenced by our limit; our limit needs to be inspiring rather than forceful. This is to say that our limit invites us to imagine how discourse is enjoyable in-itself and not incidentally as replenishment for our "indirect" relation to the ultimate truth. Theorizing is ironic toward the treatment of conversation as a means of access that opens us to the ultimate truth, because conversation is enjoyable in-itself as the work through which the interest in the development of the in-itself is embodied both as the worker's way of working out what the notion is and as his way of making explicit what he is. Man and discourse are integrated by the work of working out the in-itself. This is how "one principle takes shape in diverse ways."

Irony, then, presupposes sympathy rather than awe toward the "ultimate truth." That the ultimate truth needs discourse *and* is absolute points to a source of irony in my recognition that I am needed by the ultimate truth as much as it is needed by me. In this recognition, irony differs first from those who do not acknowledge the ultimate truth, and secondly, from those whose acknowledgment only concedes how *they* need the ultimate truth. In contrast, irony enjoys its limit, it enjoys the unfolding of the in-itself, because it enjoys being needed and used by the ultimate truth.

Enjoyment begins to describe our satisfaction as we work out the development of the notion as a way of recollecting our own identity. The movement of enjoyment begins through an act of deference to the content of the notion. The practice—deeply, the implicit and to-be-developed content of the notion—engages our interest insofar as we need to work out and make explicit what we are (as the human or discursive way of expressing the ultimate truth as subject). What we enjoy is the way in which our working out the notion in practice reinstates what we are.

We imagine that our self-identity will be worked out, realized, and made explicit through our development of the notion. The idea of confidence expresses our power to imagine this realization and our Desire to act under its auspices. It is in this sense that we acknowledge ourself to be in need, as needing to be developed and worked out. Our comfort with this need is assured by our confidence in the ultimate truth as subject and in how it depends upon us to grasp and express this as its identity.

We say that enjoyment depends upon ignorance in the sense that we exercise reserve toward our continuous need to develop ourself. The notion of ignorance suggests that while I always need to work out what I am, this need is not a lack or privation and is not itself to be worked out: It is the unshakable necessity of this need that I inherit when I am called to grasp and express the ultimate truth as subject.

Enjoyment, then, is only possible when my limit is welcomed as a necessity that needs to be demonstrated. We achieve enjoyment only insofar as we are enjoined to demonstrate—to work out and develop—our limit.

The movement of enjoyment originates in the confidence through which one gives his self to the practice because of the power to imagine that while our development of the notion first enjoins us to defer to its movement, our need to work out our identity empowers us to transform it (the notion) into a moment that we use to express the ultimate truth.

The major charge against irony is that its conception of the ultimate truth as subject or of the self-development of the notion, means that the ultimate truth for the ironist is "infinite negativity."[10] For example, for the ironist human wisdom is knowledge of ignorance (I know that I don't know), and such knowledge only delineates man as poor vis-à-vis the ultimate truth, since the best he can apparently achieve is the knowledge that he lacks this truth.

The charge might continue by saying that if knowledge of ignorance is the source of Desire, it seems as if irony originates in hatred rather than love, since it is provoked by its contempt for the ignorance of those who do not know their own ignorance. The passion of irony conceals from itself its enmity toward man (man as *multis,* as low life). The charge says that love for the Good (for the ultimate truth) that originates in negativity (hatred of man, of ignorance) cannot be good.

It is said, then, that the ironist should be pitied, since his "absolute" is the hatred of ignorance rather than his love of knowledge. Irony cannot defer to anything human; it posits the ultimate truth abstractly and makes itself the best human by implication. In this sense, the pretense of irony lies in its affirmation of something higher than man (the Good, the ultimate truth), because this affirmation *is* only by virtue of subjectivity. That is, in the absence of a positive commitment, the ultimate truth exists only by implication, by virtue of man's subjective sense of his own limitation. Thus, what irony really loves (and treats as ultimate) are the refined powers of man, e.g., to discern limitation, and what it hates is the failure of these powers to develop.

Thus, if the ironist claims to love the ultimate truth, he does not appear to defer to it in a way that permits him to be truly influenced by its development. When the root of theorizing is hatred of ignorance, theorizing cannot enjoy itself, because it acts only to replenish what is lacking. Consequently, what we aspire to can at best only be abstract unity; whereas what is needed is to reachieve theorizing as learning and, so, as enjoyable, since learning is pleasant. This is to say—theorizing must find itself good in-itself, and not because it reduces ignorance. Theorizing must accept itself as necessary and desirable and not as good by implication of its ability to reduce what is bad. One part of the charge against irony counsels that it could be tempted to be invidious, to resist developing what *it* is in-itself because it is always in danger of being distracted by its impatience toward *multis* (toward the many ways in which the ultimate truth takes shape).

To all of this irony says, "I know that I don't know," meaning that one must exercise reserve toward the ultimate truth by approaching it *through* the notion. The ultimate truth exists through its diversification into notions (discourse) and the inability to glimpse this results from treating the notion (and discourse) as oppositionally other to the ultimate truth.

Irony must enjoy itself if it is to resist the temptations of abstraction to which it is vulnerable. These temptations are raised by the challenge of treating discourse as good by implication, as a *means* to approach a remote ultimate truth: the temptation is resisted by imagining the togetherness of the ultimate truth and discourse. This power releases a man to enjoy developing the notion as an expression of the ultimate truth as subject.

Irony, then, in accepting the pleasure of deferring to the notion, still resists falling under its spell, because it knows that it must return the notion to itself as a moment in the development of the ultimate truth as subject. In the same way, the originating impulse of deference toward the notion must resist the awe toward the ultimate truth that results from its segregation from discourse in the same way that high life stands to low life.

Irony revolves into enjoyment as it grasps the need to resist dualism: on the one hand, awe for the ultimate truth and its contemptuous adaptation to discourse, or on the other hand, enchantment by the notion through the inaccessibility of the ultimate truth. Irony transforms itself into enjoyment insofar as discourse reflects into its necessary togetherness with the ultimate truth as one of its many shapes and looks.

Thus, irony develops at the moment when it has the power to laugh at the notion of the enigmatic character of the whole. It is not that irony denies the enigma, but, rather, that it laughs at the notion that the enigmatic character of the whole is a continuously problematic limit for man.

Irony, then, enjoys itself when it achieves the confidence needed to free itself from the guilt resulting from man's thinking of himself as being inadequate vis-à-vis the ultimate truth. The crime irony is often charged with, then, is that it enjoys itself because it does not find the enigmatic character of the whole a *problem* (i.e., it is not a topic for positive inquiry or theology), since it needs to begin with strength rather than with inadequacy. Irony, being free of the need to be exercised by the *problem* of enigma, has the luxury to leave that problem behind and to enjoy itself.

We ask, under what conditions does the need to work out and develop the in-itself arise? When do we need to demonstrate the essential collectedness of what belongs together? Could we say—when the ultimate truth as subject—when the in-itself—demands to be expressed, i.e., to be demonstrated? Can we say that life makes a claim that needs to be worked out and recollected?

For example, if it is perfectly clear to us that the notion and our relation to it need to be demonstrated and made explicit, it is just as certain that the need to demonstrate this very need for demonstration is a necessity that stands fast for us, a conviction we inherit with (and as) the need to glimpse and express the ultimate truth as subject. Is this not what irony sees with remarkable clarity: that the need to work out and develop is grounded in the need to defer in a way that we must accept with confidence rather than with suspicion?

NOTES

1. J. Piaget, *Moral Judgment of the Child* (London: Routledge and Keagan Paul, 1960), p. 175.

2. This resonates with Wittgenstein's notion that children are *neither* knowledgeable nor ignorant because they are not in position to be so, i.e., they are unqualified.

3. Piaget, op. cit., p. 175.

4. Besides Plato and Hegel, of course, we might think here of Wittgenstein's argument against knowing as a state of mind.

5. Albert Camus, *The Stranger*, trans. Stuart Gilbert (New York: Vintage Books, 1955), pp. 151–152.

6. Ibid., p. 9.

7. Cf. Hegel, *The Phenomenology of Mind* (New York, Harper Torchbooks, 1967), p. 80.

8. Hegel, op. cit., p. 78.

9. Klein says of Being, that it is "the most comprehensive intelligible," in J. Klein, *Plato's Trilogy*: University of Chicago Press 1977.

10. S. Kierkegaard, *The Concept of Irony*, trans. by L. Copel (New York: Harper and Row, 1965), p. 9.

Bibliography

L. Althusser, *For Marx*. London: Allan Lane, 1969.

Aristotle, *Nichomachean Ethics,* in *Introduction to Aristotle.* New York: Modern Library, 1947.

R. Barthes, *Mythologies.* London: Paladin Press, 1973.

R. Barthes, *Systeme de la Mode.* Paris: Seuil, 1967.

J. Bennett, *Rationality.* London: Routledge & Kegan Paul, 1969.

J. Bennett, *Linguistic Behavior,* New York: Cambridge University Press, 1976.

P. Berger and T. Luckmann, *Social Construction of Reality.* New York: Anchor Books, 1967.

S. Cavell, *Must We Mean What We Say.* New York: Scribner's, 1969.

N. Chomsky, *Language and Mind.* New York: Harcourt, Brace, 1968.

J. Derrida, *Speech and Phenomena.* Evanston, Ill.: Northwestern University Press, 1973.

E. Durkheim, *Rules of Sociological Method.* Glencoe; Ill.: Free Press, 1964.

H.G. Gadamer, *Philosophical Hermeneutics.* Berkeley: University of California Press, 1976.

H.G. Gadamer, *Truth and Method.* London: Sheed and Ward, 1975.

H. Garfinkel, *Studies in Ethnomethodology.* Englewood Cliffs; N.J.: Prentice-Hall, 1967.

J. Habermas, *Theorie der Geseelschaft oder Sozial Technologie.* Frankfurt: Surkhamp, 1971.

J. Habermas, *Theory and Practice,* Boston: Beacan Press, 1973.

E. Hamilton and H. Cairns, eds., *Collected Dialogues of Plato.* New York: Pantheon Books, 1966.

M. Heidegger, *Being and Time* (trans. J. Macquarrie and E. Robinson). New York: Harper & Row, 1962.

M. Heidegger, *The End of Philosophy.* New York: Harper & Row, 1973.

M. Heidegger, *Kant and the Problem of Metaphysics* (trans., J.S. Churchill). Bloomington: Indiana University Press, 1968.

E. Husserl, *The Crisis of European Sciences and Transcendental Phenomenology,* Evanston, Ill.: Northwestern University Press, 1970.

H. Innis, *The Bias of Communication.* Toronto: University of Toronto Press, 1951.

F. Jameson, *The Prison House of Language: A Critical Account of Structuralism and Russian Formalism.* Princeton, N.J.: Princeton University Press, 1977.

S. Karatheodoris, *The Logic and Ethic of Science: A Sociological Exegesis of the Cognitive Grounds of Practice and the Practical Grounds of Cognition,* Ph.D. dissertation in the Department of Sociology, New York University, 1977.

F. Kaufmann, *Methodology of the Social Sciences.* Atlantic Highlands N.J.: Humanities Press, 1944.

S. Kierkegaard, *The Concept of Irony* (trans. L.Capel) New York: Harper and Row, 1965.

J. Klein, *Plato's Trilogy,* Chicago: University of Chicago Press, 1977.

T. S. Kuhn, *Structure of Scientific Revolutions.* Chicago: University of Chicago. 1971.

I. Lakatos and A. Musgrave (eds.), *Criticism and the Growth of Knowledge.* Cambridge: Cambridge University Press, 1970.

T. Luckmann, *The Sociology of Language.* Indianapolis: Bobbs-Merrill, 1975.

K. Marx and F. Engels, *The German Ideology.* New York: International Publishers, 1947.

P. McHugh, *Defining the Situation.* Indianapolis: Bobbs-Merrill, 1968.

R. McKeon, "Philosophy and Method," *The Journal of Philosophy,* XLVIII, no. 27.

W. Outhwaite, *Understanding Social Life: The Method Called Verstehend.* New York: Holmes & Meier, 1975.

T. Parsons, *The Structure of Social Action,* New York: McGraw-Hill, 1937.

D. Pears, "Wittgenstein and Austin" in *British Analytic Philosophy,* B. Williams and A. Montefoire (eds.). London: Routledge & Kegan Paul, 1966.

J. Piaget, *Moral Judgment of the Child*. London: Routledge and Keagan Paul, 1960.

Plato, *Timaeus*.

Plato, *Apology*.

Plato, *Meno*.

R. Rorty (ed.), *The Linguistic Turn*. Chicago: University Press, 1967.

S. Rosen, *Nihilism*. New Haven, Conn.: Yale University Press, 1969.

F. de Saussure, *Course in General Linguistics*. London: Fontana/Collins, 1974.

A. Schutz, *Phenomenology of the Social World*. Evanston, Ill.: Northwestern University Press, 1967.

D. Shwayder, *The Stratification of Behavior*. Atlantic Highlands, N.J.: Humanities Press, 1968.

G. Steiner, *After Babel*. New York: Oxford University Press, 1975.

L. Strauss, *Natural Right and History*. Chicago: University of Chicago Press, 1953.

P.F. Strawson, *Meaning and Truth*. Oxford: The Clarendon Press, 1970.

F. Waismann, "Verifiability" and "Language Strata" in A. Flew (ed.), *Logic and Language*. New York: Anchor Books, 1965.

G. Warnock, *English Philosophy Since 1900*. Oxford: Oxford University Press, 1958.

M. Weber, *The Theory of Social and Economic Organization*. Glencoe; Ill.: Free Press, 1947.

P. Winch, *The Idea of a Social Science and Its Relation to Philosophy*. London: Routledge & Kegan Paul, 1958.

L. Wittgenstein, *Remarks on the Foundations of Mathematics*. Cambridge, Mass.: MIT Press, 1977.

L. Wittgenstein, *Tractatus Logico-Philosophicus*. London, 1961.

L. Wittgenstein, *Philosophical Investigations*. New York: Macmillan, 1953.

K. Wolff (ed.), *The Sociology of Georg Simmel*. Glencoe; Ill.: Free Press, 1950.

A. Wootton, *Dilemmas of Discourse*. London: Allen & Unwin Ltd., 1975.

Index